David Stark

FOR MY DEAR
FRIEND ROBERT
WITH MUCH

♡

David

David Stark

THE ART OF THE PARTY

Written with John Morse
Principal Photography by Susan Montagna
The Monacelli Press

Published in the United States in 2013
by The Monacelli Press, LLC.

Library of Congress Cataloging-in-Publication Data

Stark, David, 1968–
David Stark : the art of the party/by David Stark with John Morse ;
principal photography by Susan Montagna.
pages cm
ISBN 978-1-58093-352-0 (hardback)
1. Parties. I. Title.
GV1471.S82 2013
793.2—dc23   2012044123

Printed in China

www.monacellipress.com

10 9 8 7 6 5 4 3 2 1
First edition

Designed by Omnivore

All photography by Susan Montagna
except the following:
Daria Bishop: 72, 73, 74, 75 all, 76, 77, 80–81, 82 bottom, 83 top right, 83 bottom right, 85
Arnold Brower: 25, 28 upper right, 29
Courtesy Peter Callahan Catering: 191 bottom
Gustavo Campos: Front endpapers, 6, 26–27, 28 bottom, 28 middle left, 32–33, 41, 86, 87, 88–89 all, 119, 120–21,
122–123 all, 199, 240, back endpapers
Rick Collins: 216 all, 217 all, 218–19, 221, 222 all, 223 all, 224–25, 226–27
Aaron Delesie: Front cover, back cover, 8–21, 22 upper right, 23, 58 top, 59 bottom, 190 top
Brian Dorsey: 118, 124–25, 126 all, 127 all
Heidi Ehalt: 96, 97, 98–99 all
Billy Farrell: 202 top, 202 bottom left
Joe Kohen/Wire Image: 140 bottom
Andre Maier: 100 top, 100 bottom, 102–103
KT Merry: 58 center, 142, 143, 144–45 all, 146–47 all, 148–49, 150–51, 152 all, 153, 154 top, 154 bottom
John Parra/Wire Image: 155
Rebecca Weiss: 192, 196 top right, 197 top left

The weddings featured on pages 8–23 and 72–85 were produced in collaboration with *Martha Stewart Weddings*.

HELLO

ART is the river that runs through my life and happiness sets the course.

Every day I count my blessings that what I do is about happiness. Yes, planning and designing events is a career filled with stress and deadlines and number crunching and more juggling than a circus, but all of that energy goes toward making happiness.

It's also about making art. Our site-specific installations meld sculpture, performance, and theater—much like the Happening movement at midcentury, which organically fused art and environment into provocative amalgams.

These immersing, custom experiences are at the heart of what I do. You can, of course, take the elements of a party—food, drink, music—and toss them together like the ingredients in a salad, but it may seem just as random to your guests. With apologies to Ms. Stein, a party is a party is a party. If you only aim for adequately amusing, that's exactly what you get.

I've loved and pursued art for as long as I can remember. Art school led me eventually into floral design as a means of supporting myself while still being creative, but I soon realized that I needed broader, more evocative artistic expression.

Which brings me back to happiness. Painting in school brought me satisfaction, but my happiness was difficult to share with others in a tangible way. In event design there's always a client, which adds a new dynamic. This work requires an outside voice, will always be a collaborative process, and ideally makes a whole group of people happy at once.

All our ideas stem from this type of interpersonal connection. A party is the culmination of an extended brainstorming process. We've found that every bit of excitement we pour into the planning steps along the way blossoms when the actual event arrives.

Much of an event's energy comes from creating design opportunities out of the tiniest details and turning standard conventions on their head. Attention to detail is what guests walk away with: an invite that moves beyond the functional piece of paper to become a mini work of art, an escort card disguised as a party favor, the waitstaff outfitted in ceremonial garb.

Those layers of detail are what set our events apart and what people find astounding. We've learned to plant surprises, big and small, that unfold as an event progresses and as guests move around. This delivers a sense of discovery that keeps the party energized and keeps guests intrigued.

A party is not about decoration. Anyone can stuff a room floor to ceiling with orchids. It's not about the money. Money can't buy love and it can't buy fun. Parties are about experience. Create an event that turns the evening into living theater, bringing the guests into the play not as audience, but as actors, just as those Happenings of the 1950s and '60s did.

When there's joy in every detail, that happiness is passed along to the client and, in turn, to the guests who carry that happiness home—a gift more precious than any swag bag could ever deliver.

This book, too, was a process. Yes, we've packed it with plenty of dazzling photographs of the end product: glamorous fêtes fit for royalty. But we've also pulled the curtain back to offer a sneak peek behind the scenes, an examination of not just where we go, but how we get there. How from one gold nugget of an idea, perhaps something as simple as a childhood summer memory, we mine a mother lode of rare and precious jewels.

The steps we take are a precise ballet involving not just goals and plans but also the dozens in our crew who can literally take trash—old catalogs, paint swatches, you name it—and turn it into treasure. You'll see.

And like any good party, this book is also a lively celebration. A hearty, delicious portion of design and décor is offered for each event, explaining the underpinnings of our design decisions and bringing the art and joy of the party to life. You might even say this book itself is the life of the party.

From Manhattan skyscrapers to Turkish palaces, from picnics on the lawn to sit-down dinners for a thousand, we invite you to drop in on and participate in some of the most exciting parties we've had the honor to design.

So join us as we dive into what makes a party—and this career—tick. You are cordially invited!

THE journey is the destination. That trusty adage rings true for so many situations, including parties.

Appreciating all the moments leading up to a big event cultivates a sense of satisfaction that lets a party blossom. Like planting a garden, it's an organic process that needs careful nurturing along the way. Sure, harvest time is rewarding, but any gardener worth his topsoil will tell you that the joy of a garden is gardening. Relishing the process every step of the way makes the fruit taste that much sweeter.

For events, that means paying attention to so-called little things. As Michelangelo said, "Trifles make perfection and perfection is no trifle." And he should know. What makes the Sistine Chapel the, well . . . the Sistine Chapel of art is not only that it's an enormous masterpiece, it's that every detail in it is masterful.

A gracious home in Detroit framed a masterpiece of a wedding we planned in coordination with the mother of the bride, a woman who personifies good taste. She put every speck of her talent to work making her daughter's day the very definition of a fairy-tale wedding.

One of the most outstanding features of the big day was what it wasn't. No bling, no ceilings dripping with orchids, not a hint of ostentation. The groomsmen took a pass on tuxedos and dressed up in seersucker, a sartorial choice in tune with the sultry June air. It was a common-sense selection that worked because it fit—a guiding principle for any event. Yes, the couple could have rented the grand ballroom in a fine hotel anywhere in the world. But why? Here was a beautiful home surrounded by a beautiful garden with a beautiful bride at the center of a beautiful day. All we needed or wanted to do was accentuate all that beauty.

Not everyone owns a grand manor, but any home that is filled with love and personality and at least a small patch of space in case dancing breaks out can host a successful event. It all depends on assessing your assets and making the most of them. From the moment guests arrived at the wedding, everywhere they looked and with each step they took, they experienced style and comfort, quality and elegance, and, most of all, happiness.

The bride wore the dress her mother wore, which was the dress *her* mother wore. The bridal bouquet was tied in lace that belonged to the bride's great-grandmother. The cake was made in the home's kitchen. These gentle, easy, lovely touches can work for anyone, even on the tightest budget.

The contents of gift bags left in each guest's hotel room were made in the home and the bags were filled in the home, too. If guests found the granola inside extra yummy maybe it's because it, too, was homemade. Even if no one realized all or even any of these details, the fact that such personal touches were behind every aspect of the day helped to imbue the event with personality. Design details and decisions like these are well within anyone's reach. These touches started off a day made for memories, the sort of perfect thing money can't buy—like love.

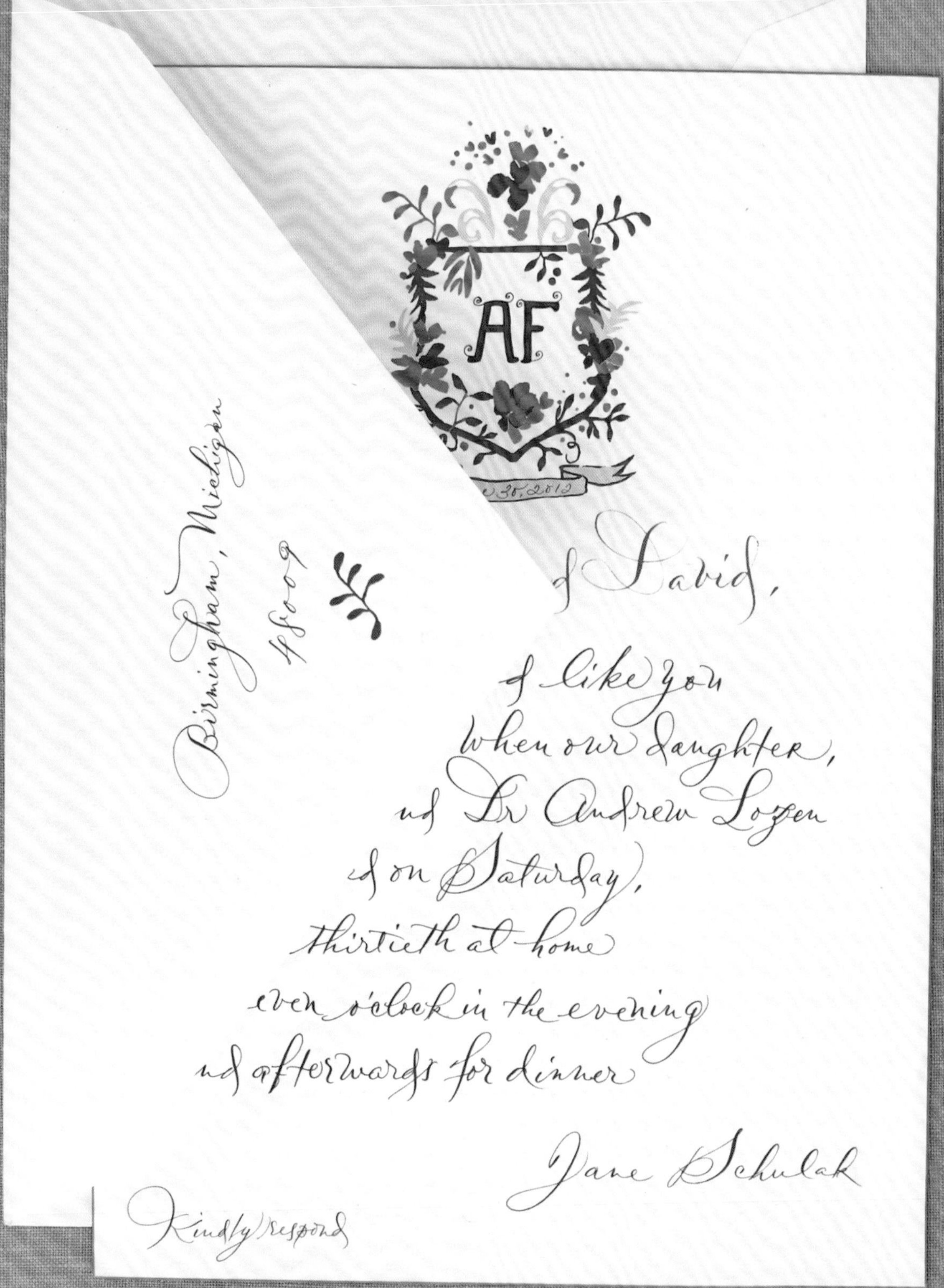
AF
30, 2012
Birmingham, Michigan
48009
d David,
d like you
when our daughter,
nd Dr Andrew Lozen
d on Saturday,
thirtieth at home
even o'clock in the evening
nd afterwards for dinner
Jane Schulak
Kindly respond

Opposite: The invitation fuses the couple's crest, designed by Happy Menocal, and the calligraphy of Bernard Maisner to mix formal and relaxed elements, just like the event itself. Protocol says that an invitation should never carry a personalized message, but these attendance requests were so individualized, so effective, they rose above the rule. Parties are living events. Don't let rules nail you down.

Left: An oversized golden egg, casually situated as though a giant hen had left it in the vegetable patch, adds a whimsical complement to the garden's sculptures and provides another fairy-tale moment of surprise and delight for guests wending their way through the grounds.

Two 13-foot-tall topiary chickens—inspired by the animal lawn sculptures crafted by French artists Les Lalanne, some of which the owners already had in the yard—stand sentinel at the arrival gate. Delightfully quirky yet refined in form, they set a tone of elegance and fun that immediately put guests at ease.

Opposite: A tipped-over "paint can" spilling a velvety overflow of pink peonies and roses subtly directs guests toward the main ceremony space.

Below: A short walk down a path "sprouting" daisies leads to a garden room known as the Sheep Courtyard, named for a trio of Les Lalanne ovine sculptures. Above its hedge, a band strummed a lute and played a flute from a tree house built into the low branches of a towering oak.

The seat of each chair held a folded paper fan tied with a sprig of lavender to provide guests with a hint of fragrance as they fanned away the late-afternoon heat. The bride's bouquet, created with blossoms that looked as if they'd been gathered from the family's garden, was tied with a piece of lace from her great-grandmother's gown—a gentle touch that guests might not have noticed but that meant much to the bride, her mother, and grandmother.

Right and above: Glimpses of color add surprising splashes of jeweled hues throughout the day. Sumptuous treats from Olivier Cheng Catering including vivid green, cucumber-mint martinis are passed around by easy-on-the-eyes waiters dressed in pink, orange, and baby-blue jackets made in Italy and designed to complement the wedding décor. For dessert, the young men donned white pants and sailor shirts to serve up trays of sweets in a rainbow of colors. Meanwhile, all-white lawn furniture let the lush green of the grounds speak for itself.

Opposite: Adorned with tiny blooms and *fraises des bois* plucked straight from the garden, a chocolate wedding cake, baked in the home's kitchen from a favorite family recipe, reveled in a confident simplicity.

The tablecloth material—bright, white cotton from France printed with whimsical, strewn flowers— translated to several other of the wedding's unique design moments, including the form of the crest on the invitations and the floral arrangements.

An air-conditioned dinner tent—hidden behind a tall temporary hedge made of sculpted box-wood—included six large paper chandeliers inspired by the tablecloth's flowery whimsy.

After speeches, a band performed in front of a starry night backdrop à la Van Gogh, with cake cutting leading to a night of dancing in one of the home's stunning galleries. The lawn outside, bordered on its far side by a swimming pool, became the dessert room and de facto hang-out space. Overhead, a real starry night looked down on the proceedings.

23

SO YOU WANT TO HAVE A PARTY...

THERE's not any one best reason to have a party, but there should always be *a* reason. It's a simple concept, but one missed surprisingly often. Sometimes the reason is obvious. The main reason for a wedding is of course to get married and to share that ceremony of commitment with the meaningful people in your life. But just because it's obvious doesn't mean those involved can't get lost in the peripheral details of planning their special day. When the bride and groom worry about matching the bridesmaids' dresses to the tablecloths to the napkins and the groom dithers over whether his best man might have an allergy to his gardenia boutonnière, it's time for a reality check.

Similarly, when a nonprofit hosts a fund-raiser, the organizing committee often starts by plowing into a possible theme, the guest list, canapés, cash bar vs. open bar, and so on. They sometimes forget the primary purpose of a fund-raiser—to raise funds. The top priority of the evening is to make money, as much as humanly possible. There'll be other goals—rewarding big supporters, cultivating new friends, connecting people socially, honoring a special guest, grabbing some media attention—but keeping your eye on the main prize makes it that much easier to get all those other ducks in a row.

Once the major outlines of the party—budget, date, scouting a location, guest count, etc.—have been established, then go on to the details. Some are fun—who doesn't like to pick out the flowers for the centerpieces?—and some simply sniggling but still important, like determining a seating chart that will foster just the right amount of frisson to keep things interesting between guests.

Write down your goals. Whether it's a small birthday party or a huge corporate event, the overarching rule of setting a goal is as important as ever. And while everyone wants to host a "fun" event, it's okay to acknowledge an ulterior motive. Maybe it's to launch a new campaign. Maybe it's to celebrate a corporate or personal milestone. Maybe a company just wants to polish its halo. Sometimes it's all three.

Target accomplished that hat trick—and so much more—when it joined with the National Education Association's Read Across America organization, a nonprofit dedicated to promoting childhood literacy, to reach out to students in kindergarten through third grade. The effort fit nicely with Target's self-imposed good citizenship commitment to return 5 percent of their profits directly back into local community-building organizations. Target's event celebrated a large donation to Read Across America and launched a five-year program to help participating students reach that literacy goal.

We began with an outsized sculpture on the venerated steps of the New York Public Library's main branch, a historic institution and the embodiment of the universal ideals that literacy is a right and that reading forms the cornerstone of any vibrant democracy.

There, between the library's imposing lion sculptures 20-foot-tall letters spelling out R-E-A-D, crafted from 15,000 Dr. Seuss books, reached into the sky. That staggering temporary sculptural installation made notoriously jaded New Yorkers—who pass the landmark by the thousands every hour—stop in their tracks and take notice. Beyond its artistic and communicative task of introducing the full event, the elements of the sculpture also served a secondary purpose: the books were later distributed to local libraries across America.

We met our goals of helping Target help a great cause, but the best endorsement was the smiles of ten-year-olds!

Fifteen thousand Dr. Seuss books create an imperative that stopped traffic on Fifth Avenue. The volumes inside were donated to libraries around the country when the temporary installation came down.

Who rea
We ea

art of Targe
nt to educat
Dr. Se
lebration

Free

In front of a gaggle of TV crews and reporters, a wonderful band of personalities from stage and screen—including Uma Thurman, Mark Ruffalo, and entertainer Common—used an oversized pair of scissors to cut a bright ribbon in front of the main sculpture. This inaugurated a fantasy of festivities inside the library, where they then read to the children from a stage featuring huge blow-ups of the books' famous illustrations.

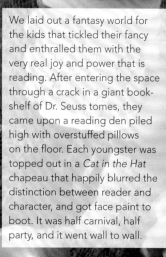

We laid out a fantasy world for the kids that tickled their fancy and enthralled them with the very real joy and power that is reading. After entering the space through a crack in a giant book-shelf of Dr. Seuss tomes, they came upon a reading den piled high with overstuffed pillows on the floor. Each youngster was topped out in a *Cat in the Hat* chapeau that happily blurred the distinction between reader and character, and got face paint to boot. It was half carnival, half party, and it went wall to wall.

A METHOD TO THE MADNESS

IT'S A RULE: The more easy-breezy a party looks, the more work it requires behind the scenes. Like an amusement park ride that makes riders feel as if they could fly off the rail at any given moment, delivering a thrill requires the ultimate in engineering skill. You have to know what you're doing.

Parties should feel fun and have a sense of the madcap, but paradoxically, creating a happy-go-lucky mood takes a methodology. Using an adding machine or tape measure to plan is not really anyone's idea of fun. But if you want to have event success, you have to invest in the nitty-gritty first.

The most basic element of a party's physical design, and the one I execute first, is planning the space. All other design decisions will flow from that. A grid on a piece of paper with proper dimensions for the floor will do. Fill in all the metrics: number of guests, type of food and/or drink, entertainment, possible dancing space, etc. Each of these elements requires actual physical space.

Apply those nuts-and-bolts basics to every aspect of planning—particularly the budget. If you want centerpieces that are "lush spring bouquets," then imagine a perfect concoction, say, of six peonies, twelve garden roses, fifteen tulips, and six stems of lilacs. Then price out each stem, add in container costs and the time it takes to put together each bouquet, multiply by the number of tables and—voila!—you have your budget for centerpieces. Also remember to look at the size of the table and the size of the bouquet and make sure it's a good physical fit. No guest will ever look at a centerpiece and notice that calculation. But you must take time to suss it out or you will end up with too many arrangements or too few, they'll be too big or too small, you'll go over budget, or you won't have enough time to put it all together. Every guest will notice *those* miscalculations. Make choices proactively at the design stage, not when your credit card maxxes out.

One easy way to stay within budget is to use low-cost materials, especially unexpected items. We've built our firm's reputation on expertly manipulating inexpensive materials into fantastic décor elements. When we created the bi-annual fund-raiser for the American Patrons of the Tate Museum, we selected colored pencils as our focal point. Since the fund-raiser honors both art and artists, the pencils made for a happy metaphor and, when lined up by the thousands in undulating waves down long rectangular tables or rung around glass containers in the middle of round tables, they became bright, amusing style elements.

This epitomizes a significant rule of design: you can harness the intrinsic beauty of inexpensive materials if you invest time and labor to transform them into an object of beauty. Just remember that when you calculate your material costs, you must also budget something for your time.

Which brings us to the budgeting of time itself. Every party has a schedule—put every phase of a party on it. This goes so far as planning when to decide what to put on the invite, when to determine who will get the invite, when to order the invite, when to mail the invite. Remember that every design decision is also a time decision.

Organization is critical, to be sure, and a schedule not only keeps you on track, it keeps you calm and in control during the creative process—a key to enjoying the actual event!

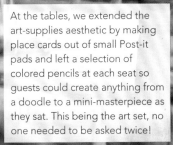

At the tables, we extended the art-supplies aesthetic by making place cards out of small Post-it pads and left a selection of colored pencils at each seat so guests could create anything from a doodle to a mini-masterpiece as they sat. This being the art set, no one needed to be asked twice!

To create this look, we measured the width of each pencil, then calculated the exact length of the undulating base that ran down the center of each rectangular table. Using two-sided carpet tape, we adhered thousands of pencils, one by one, until every table had its brilliantly colored centerpiece. After the event, the tape allowed us to deconstruct all the centerpieces without harming the pencils, which were donated to an arts group.

CREATE AN ORIGINAL

A party begins as an empty canvas. Whether an empty tent or living room, a reception hall or a poolside retreat, any event space is just waiting to be filled with an experience.

When you create an event, you become an artist. Whatever artists can imagine they can paint on a canvas—the key is being able to imagine it first. A vivid imagination opens the door to originality. At the point of creation the possibilities are as limitless as the imagination. Without imagination, however, you'll likely just end up with a copy of what's already been done.

That's how Warhol could create a portrait of Marilyn—a face the public had seen countless times—and make it like something they had never seen before. The vast majority of the art you see on walls falls into the category of copies, forgettable imagery that looks like everything else. Can you even recall what the "art" in the last hotel room you stayed at looked like?

It's the same for events. Jumbo shrimp, open bars, fancy surroundings, or any other delight only go so far toward making them memorable. Without imaginative touches, guests won't remember an event any more than a middle-of-the-road poster.

Two different parties that used the same tent are good illustrations of how to give visual voice to originality. Each allowed us to paint a party straight out of the imagination. And though we used the same structure for both events, the two experiences were entirely different. This tent is home to a number of parties at Lincoln Center, New York's magisterial, mesmerizing mecca of the performing arts—it's also one of the few places in the city cavernous enough to comfortably seat a thousand diners.

One event revolved around a gala supporting the American Associates of the National Theatre following a production of *War Horse*. Taking our cue from the play itself, we created a party that captured a fanciful moment during a scene, a snapshot of those regal, heady months before England entered World War I—a moment in time epitomized by social graces, urbane elegance, and fashionable world-weariness. Yet what we created was an original homage that evoked the play without stooping to parody.

Outsized portraits of fin-de-siècle British royalty in trompe-l'œil, gilded frames look out over the 650 guests who were transported to *War Horse*'s era for the evening.

An empty party tent—the event planner's ultimate blank canvas—awaiting transformation.

Tables adorned with place settings alternately featuring small Union Jacks or Old Glories, strings of twinkly lights crisscrossed with lines of jaunty pennants stamped in Liberty of London flower prints, and maypoles adorned with wide ribbons that unspooled out and across the entire space alluded to the serene gentility of the Empire's glory days.

Opposite: About midway through dinner, the elaborate two-man mechanical puppet of the horse at the center of *War Horse* took a high-stepped trot right through the middle of the tables to great applause from the diners.

Details from Hans Holbein the Younger's portraits of Henry VIII's courtiers and Gothic Perpendicular window frames reinterpreted in stained-glass-like transparency peered over diners. The tables were set as if they were scenes from a Dutch still life, with plump, glistening fruit interspersed with bowls filled with cascades of large roses.

THE same tent took on an entirely different personality when it hosted one of the most sought-after invitations on the New York social calendar—the dinner following opening night of the Metropolitan Opera. In recent years, the Met has commissioned a new production of a work to launch each season; this year it debuted *Anna Bolena*, a retelling of the life of Henry VIII's doomed wife. Again we honored the stunning originality of the work by complementing it with our own original creation, one that deferred to it without relying on expected Tudor tchotchkes.

All the décor referenced the opera, yet there wasn't a hint of imitation. A low-rent version of the performance—still fresh on the mind of the 1,100 guests who had just seen it—would have come as a let-down. Instead, we let the event extend the evening's romance and drama, albeit with a much happier ending than poor Anne's.

Thick rings of lights hanging from chains befitting a castle burnish the room with an amber glow. Around the room, chandeliers holding dozens of tall pillar candles stand sentry.

SO INVITING

IF parties are the feature presentation, invitations are the movie trailer.

The invitation answers the crucial basics: What's the occasion? What's the time and place? What's the dress? But it also answers the less obvious questions that naturally come to a guest's mind: Does the party look fun? Is it worth my time? What can I expect?

Invitations must excite the mind, whet the appetite, and beckon the recipient. And just like an effective movie trailer, they must make you want to go to the coming attraction. Not every party needs an invite, of course. If you're throwing together an informal dinner, just pick up the phone and see who's up for your famous meatloaf. If you're putting together a night of poker, send out e-mails and aim to muster a quorum. But make no mistake—an honest-to-goodness event requires an honest-to-goodness invitation.

We see invites as the first reveal of a party's decorative motif. A party that aims to be edgy requires an invite that makes you look twice. A formal affair lends itself to a buttoned-down invitation. Never over-promise on the invite. If someone gets a glittering, three-paneled, oversized card that showers confetti when you pull it out of the envelope—that said, please don't ever put confetti in an envelope, it's just annoying—then that party better be a blow-out featuring a disco ball over a roller rink with Gloria Gayner blaring over the sound system.

Never confuse with the invite. If the font is Edwardian script, engraved on 200-pound, gold-tipped card stock requesting guests arrive at seven o'clock, they'll rightfully expect something closer to Beluga on delicate blinis and flowing champagne than pigs in a blanket and a cash bar.

I am a strict believer in printed and mailed invitations. Taking the time to send a card shows your guests you care. Just do it if at all possible. The TLC exuded by a printed invitation is also enhanced by a thoughtful design that visually speaks directly to the affair. When we were asked to create an intimate baby shower luncheon for a young Hollywood starlet, we knew we were dealing with an event that would be a world away from cotton candy pinks and ridiculous games that no guest really wants to play.

Instead, our young mom-to-be decided on a palette based on the colors of the baby's nursery—chocolate browns and golden yellows—that were a far cry from stereotypical baby pastels. That simple and refreshing selection, which served as the invite's color scheme, informed guests they could look forward to an afternoon of sophisticated pleasure long before they stepped into the lush garden setting of a sumptuous Los Angeles backyard. A tiny elephant on the invite hinted that there would be plenty of fun, too.

The invitation's color story came to full glory at the luncheon table, where little buttons of chamomile sat next to tight bouquets of sunflowers interspersed among wee sprigs of grasses and garden roses, a gentle floral selection that looked freshly gathered from the nearby garden.

This being Hollywood, the happy couple decided they would keep their choice for a baby's name on the down low by using an alias—Mac—as the real name's stand-in on an invitation created by Cheree Berry. One can only imagine they were preparing for the day when little Mac would be checking into the Chateau Marmont under his very own assumed name in a clever ploy to deflect the paparazzi!

Baby **MAC** is on his way...

As a surprise for Ali,
we would be grateful if you would choose a book
with special meaning for Baby Mac's future library.
Please pen a note on the enclosed book plate
and place it on the inside cover so that he
will always know why this book was chosen for him.

xo

Given with love by

Since both the guest of honor
and Target share a dedication to
charities that help new mothers,
their "maternal bonding" led
to the company serving as an
unofficial co-host for the event.
The elephant concept on the
invitation popped up again as a
herd of cutout elephants stood
guard over a table that held
shaped escort cards noting table
assignments.

55

Starched white linen napkins at place settings cradled small hand-carved elephants holding each guest's name card. The little wooden pachyderms also served as the guests' parting gifts. Bottles formerly destined for the recycling bin were covered in spirals of twine and string and paired with wooden and ceramic containers, creating a small trove of tabletop finds that looked as though they had been plucked from an international bazaar.

A host's responsibility doesn't end when a guest gets a drink in hand. The host's duty is to make each guest feel comfortable, welcome, and happy for the entire event—including during dining. Thoughtful seating assignments promote effervescent conversation, introduce new friends, and add vigor by gently nudging people to break out of their usual cliques.

Every seated meal benefits when the host tells people, even if verbally, where to sit. It shows you took time to think about them as you planned your event and saves the guests the awkwardness of fumbling around and negotiating with others for space. "Just sit any-where," translates roughly to, "I'm careless . . . just wait until you taste the pot roast . . . you'll see."

Consider how two new people may interact. Aim to stimulate happy conversation. Help the shy break out of their shell. Make the gregarious take pause and listen for a change. Assigned seats are especially important when guests don't know each other; thoughtful placement could lead to a new friendship, even if it only lasts from the salad through dessert.

Split up couples! At least have them sit across from or at an angle to each other, to offer them a chance to chat with someone new. Every couple secretly appreci-ates a little break from their regular diet. The same goes for other types of tight social connections as well, such as business associates. Ever gone to a dinner, sat next to a coworker, and felt like it just extended your work day by three hours? Not fun.

Large events need table assignments most. Stop Uncle Clem sitting across from Cousin Ed and spend-ing the evening regaling all within earshot about the time they dated twin sisters who turned out to be she-bears.

Don't force seat assign-ments if the event is super-casual. If you are serving buffet-style chili and expect everyone to find a spot in the living room to sit and watch the game, you can hardly put a place card in the center of a sofa. Match the degree of formality to the occasion.

SEAT assignments offer the absolute best hope for making the most of every guest's energy and, in turn, ensure each has the best experience possible. Make a basic floor chart with each table drawn into place. Using two different colors of Post-It notes, assign one color to men and the other to women. Write each guest's name on a note. Move the notes around until you find a good balance. For a large party, tape them down just in case a sudden gale-force wind blows your whole arrangement away!

Traditional etiquette calls for a folded, tent place card just above each plate, at twelve o'clock. But this is the twenty-first century: use this necessary detail to turn something ordinary into the extraordinary. A hang tag branded with the guest's name, for instance, can be tied around the napkin. A name beautifully painted in calligraphy onto a stone makes a sweet memento of the event for guests to take home.

There are those who don't understand seat assignments and think they're fascist. You might catch them sneaking in to switch place cards before dinner, tipping a chair forward over the table to indicate it's taken, or even piling hats or jackets on chairs to stake claims. They're worse than impolite. They're just plain tacky. It's not the California Gold Rush, people, it's dinner. As a host, there's not much you can do except pretend their unfortunate behavior doesn't bother you—and not invite them back.

Having no seating plan opens the door to a dull evening. Without it, the four guests who drove to an event together will more likely than not end up sitting next to each other at dinner, talking about much the same things they discussed on the ride up. On the way home, they'll also only be able to share stories about how strange it was that no one from the party would talk to *them*!

The Well-Mannered Table

RESOLVE TO SOLVE

WAS there ever a more cleverly deceptive painter than Matisse? So many of his light, charming paintings look like an afternoon of play with brush and palette—a dab here, a swoosh there, perhaps a racy chablis at his side. What fun!

In reality, of course, the master poured endless hours into his expressive canvases; every stroke of color, form, nuance, shadow, and light is studied and executed to perfection. He only *makes* it look easy.

That's the goal for parties, too. We want guests to slip into our events like they're dipping into a silken bubble bath. We want décor that looks perfect in every detail, even if we installed only an hour before. When the band strikes up, we want it to feel as natural as a mockingbird announcing dusk with song.

Setting up a party is like building a house of cards: it's a delicate dance of layering level upon structured level skillfully. First comes lighting, then the install, then tables are wheeled in, set, and on and on. Usually you're working inside a pressure cooker, in a battle against time and space, sometimes rushing into an empty location at six knowing guests dine at eight. But of course there's always the chance that Murphy's Law will come into play.

Say you have an event on the forty-seventh floor and you have to share the one and only freight elevator with all the other service personnel in that skyscraper. Maybe you plan a floral outlay befitting the Rose Bowl Parade and a sudden frost kills off your supply. Or your space is in the penthouse of the hotel across the street from the United Nations . . . the day the President is coming to town to address the General Assembly. Try talking your way around that roadblock! We've experienced it all.

Events are filled with perishables—flowers, food, ice—but nothing is as fragile as time. Setting up an event, time dwindles down like the candles in the "Pit and the Pendulum," so bright and welcoming when first lit, so dim and foreboding as they flicker out.

With a party, your one and only option is to meet your commitment. That means thinking on your feet, confronting the task, and, most important, keeping cool. If things don't go right during the process, there are any number of ways to get perspective. Walk around the block. Get a cup of coffee. Make a phone call about an entirely unrelated project. Eat an apple (not a candy bar). Take a deep breath. The diversion gets your mind off the problem. Even if a break takes only two minutes, it will help you come back refreshed and sharpen your focus.

When you first calculate your prep time, double it. Say that under normal circumstances, a wine run will take thirty minutes. Plan an hour. Do your shopping the day before. Whatever can be accomplished ahead of time, do. You will make Matisse proud.

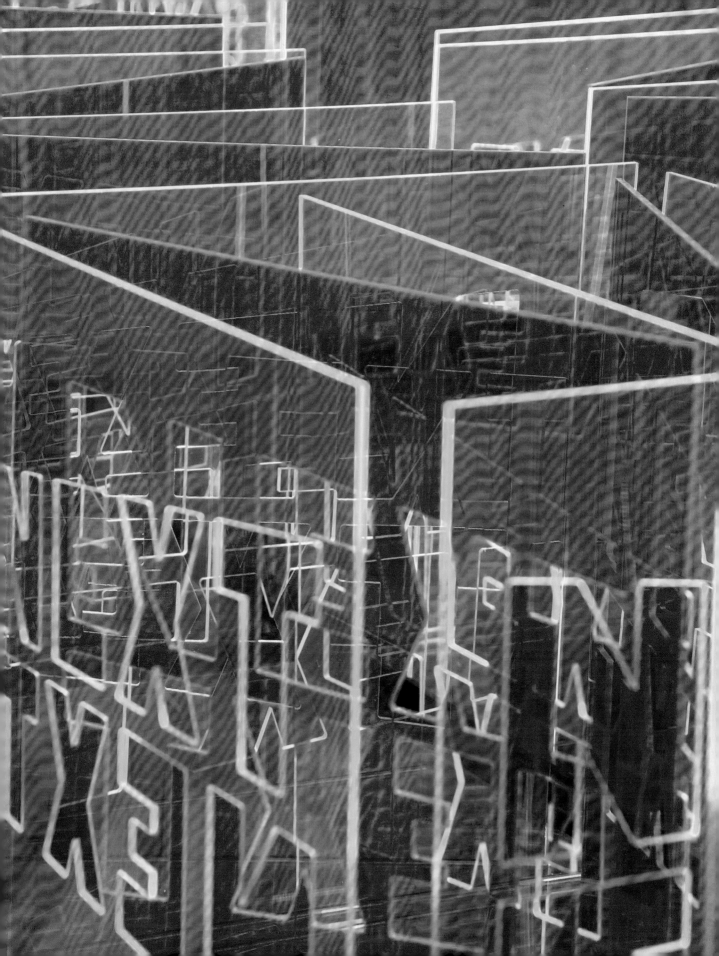

Nothing so pointedly epitomizes the battle against Murphy's Law as our fund-raiser for the American Friends of the Israel Museum. The museum wanted to emphasize its rich heritage of showcasing cutting-edge works as their event's design touchstone, so it chose "ART NEXT" as the theme for the evening. On the invitation, whooshing streams of light and color behind the lettering made it look as though the words were rushing to the paper's surface. So spectacular was the design, we decided to create an enormous reproduction of the word "NEXT" as it appeared on the invite, framed in welded steel and suspended high above the gala.

We precut thousands of yards of fluorescent green flagging tape—the bright plastic ribbon used around construction sites—and organized them for easy attachment to the edges of each letter once we arrived on site. We laid out the letters in the space and unwound the thousands of pieces of tape, stretched out each length, and set them in careful rows. The crew of riggers we hired to lift the letters into place were instructed not to touch a single thing until we gave them the "go." Maybe we weren't clear enough. In one fateful moment, we took our eyes off the display and, with a misstep here, a dragged ladder there—in an instant!—thousands of feet of thousands of strands, more than eight miles total, became a monstrous rat's nest of tangle. Suddenly our installation agenda had a brand new, most pressing priority: unknotting miles and miles of tape.

Once successfully suspended, the tape draped up and away from the letters high into the ceiling, a three-dimensional interpretation of the two-dimensional paper invitation's image.

DETAILS make a party. They can unmake one, too.

Mine is a service industry, so I must do what the client wants, even if it's something I think runs counter to the best interests of the event. One client, to cite an achingly unfortunate example, wanted to extend the party's design theme to specially printed toilet paper.

The problem wasn't just the stratospheric level of naucheness or a case of a metaphor gone awry—and boy, did it ever. It was simply too much detail. If you find yourself obsessing over picayune bits, step back, regroup, and take it down a notch. Cramming as many takes on a theme as possible into limited time and space isn't impressive. It's clutter.

When one of America's most famous domestic doyennes asked us to plan her nephew's wedding to his beau at her beautiful estate in upstate New York, we relished the opportunity to create the opposite type of party, a truly classy event. It was to be the ultimate picnic luncheon party—with a wedding thrown in—as relaxed as it was elegant, as flawless as it was simple. When you create an event, you don't need a lot of stuff. You need the right stuff. This is especially true when the setting is already spectacular.

This was casually chic meets *The Great Gatsby*. In a broad courtyard in front of the estate's massive gray stone horse barn, seventy-five guests sat on rows of white bentwood chairs. The grooms entered from each side, meeting in the middle to exchange vows. The hostess's pooch, a tidy garland around its neck, served as flower dog. A much larger matching garland, tucked into the arch above the barn's towering wood doors, framed the couple. A small ensemble including a violinist accompanied the ceremony.

After the "I do's," everyone strolled through the garden to the estate's sprawling lawn. Cocktails were served as the guests dispersed among the panoply of engaging diversions, including lawn darts, horseshoes, and badminton. For those without the inclination to dabble in those splendid pastimes, picnic blankets dotted the grass, each outfitted with a low table of flowers, crudités and nut cups, and a cold bottle of wine, a set of glasses at the ready. Plump pillows invited guests to sit, lean, or even recline. The plush lawn practically begged people to untie their wing tips—and who could blame them if they caught a catnap beneath the shade of one of the estate's apple trees?

The party worked because it fit the setting. High collars, gilded chandeliers, a big band—all of these are fine in the right time and place, but this event was never meant to be grandiose. The party was a knockout not because it was at an estate, but because it was at a true home. The blessing of this event was not the grand stone paddock, it was the love and tenderness reflected in the day's details, the sort of things that could make any backyard a place you want to be. This was a fantasy picnic come to life, where you barely needed to lift a finger to have a good time, save plucking the occasional grape from its bunch.

The wedding featured greenery that looked like we had just scooped it out of the adjoining garden—a celebration of the intrinsic elegance in nature's simplest offerings.

Guests were encouraged to roam the estate and engage in a variety of amusing diversions, which also created spontaneous interactions—and sometimes even a smidge of wooing. This was a wedding, after all!

Colored-glass bottles and other small collectables arranged in compact clusters and vintage medicine bottles and little earthen jugs holding single stems of grasses and flowers make for design accents neither overwrought nor overthought; bell jars hold still-life arrangements that look as though they have been pulled straight from the hostess's summer kitchen. If you want your party to convey a sense of straightforward ease, use straightforward, easy elements.

A sprinkle of small "rooms" furnished in wicker, each different from the others, stretch across the lawn, making for visual harmony without visual repetition.

A buffet luncheon from Peter Callahan Catering served on gracious china allowed guests to sit wherever they chose—not a seating chart in sight. Some found chairs, others took to blankets scattered across the lawn à la Seurat's *A Sunday Afternoon on the Island of La Grande Jatte*. It was that kind of setting: luxurious and splendid accoutrements adrift in a coolly casual sea.

PARTY TO THE PEOPLE

THE world needs more parties. That doesn't necessarily mean late-night blowouts powered by music and laughter and tiny bubbles tickling your nose—though can there really ever be too many of those?

Parties should seep into more parts of our daily lives in ways big and small. Why shouldn't a mariachi band play while you're waiting at the DMV? What's wrong with having canapés when you visit the dry cleaner? A party atmosphere should be infused into as many potential venues as possible, including stores. Shopping should be fun, not a chore. So we decided to create a party that didn't look like a party and a store that didn't look like a store, blurring the line so completely that shopping and partying melded into an entirely new experience, a retail event far greater than the sum of its parts. Our firm helped pioneer "pop-up" stores, retail outlets that suddenly appear in a temporary location to generate excitement and then, just as quickly, disappear. Our goal has evolved, however. We now take the notion of a temporary store one step farther—to tweak it with a dash of bash and cross the idea of a concept store with an art installation.

In one instance we ambushed design store Haus Interior in New York's NoLIta neighborhood for one month. To start, we cleared out all the usual merchandise and replaced it with an environment that invited visitors to step through the looking glass and into the captivating whir of a party playground.

Inspired by the hand-hewn goodness of a woodworker's atelier, our store, WoodShop, delightfully twisted the notion of a retail outlet into a party confection just familiar enough to make it welcoming and just edgy enough to make it an entirely new adventure. A visit to the store had to be about more than the experience, though. Like all parties, it needed substance. So we made sure we provided unique wares available for a wide range of budgets, with a concentration on things you weren't likely to find at the store next door.

Some things were functional, such as pencils, wooden vases, and wooden paintbrushes made into wall clocks. Others were simply madcap, such as wooden cupcakes, wooden phones, and other quirky items without a use in the world save your more whimsical pursuits. And like parties, couldn't the world use a little more of that?

The intimate displays created from inexpensive materials had resonance precisely because they were humble and homemade—impersonal and expensive you can buy in any store. There was nothing mass-market about these simple glimpses of character and charm.

Not every item in the shop was timber-centric—we also sold soft pillows, napkins, table runners—but most of the store looked like a forest of wares.

Traditionally utilitarian or mundane objects were recast, as if by a carpenter with a serious sense of whimsy.

Since we set up shop for the month of February, many items revolved around a theme of love and hearts. Among the most popular items was a box of "chocolates," which offered a selection of different woods hewn into bite-sized "truffles."

The truck's vertical proportion was particularly important: when working in the out-of-doors, you must command a space by making a very tall statement.

A visit to the Windy City let us take another party to the streets. Inspired by the American architectural vernacular perfectly exemplified by the giant donut sign at Randy's Donuts in Los Angeles, we disguised a street vendor's truck as an enormous Target shopping bag filled with gargantuan fruits and vegetables crafted from carved foam. It landed like a one-float parade in the plaza in front of the famed Chicago Tribune Building, one of the city's busiest pedestrian crossroads. Announcing that the retailer now offered fresh produce in its aisles, this street happening—which we later staged in Washington, Seattle, and Austin—created a party for thousands where no one needed an invitation. Guests just showed up or ran smack-dab into it when they least expected it. Now that's a nice surprise.

Fresh Has Arrived.
Your Target Now Has Fresh Grocery.

Our gracious hostess, Giada de Laurentiis, helped people to stop and linger in our chosen location. With cooking demonstrations, book signings, and her charming repartee, she gave the event warmth and helped draw foot traffic—we were able to give away 10,000 bags of fresh produce and thousands of seed packets to onlookers.

FOR MAYOR! PASTA FOR EVERYONE!!!

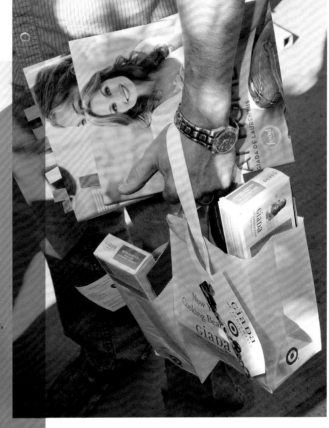

KIEHL's, the venerated skin and hair care company, began business with a corner apothecary in New York's East Village in 1851, near the corner where Dutch governor Peter Stuyvesant planted a pear tree that lived for three hundred years. Yet there is nothing old-fashioned about the company's marketing savvy—it launched Andy Warhol's favorite blue astringent in 1964 and paired with artist Jeff Koons in 2010 for a limited-edition product collection.

That flair for embracing the new continued when Kiehl's asked us to figure out an innovative way to introduce a small group of visiting female Asian press editors to their products. We could have had everyone sit in rows and watch a PowerPoint demonstration, but where's the party in that? Instead we took the women on a tour of the product lines staged as a visit to a scandalous underground speakeasy. Our setting was—*wait for it*—a bar that once was an 1890s private men's club of a certain stripe that practically invented the Sunday morning walk of shame and a scandalous underground speakeasy.

Delivering our guests to the sidewalk-level entrance, a "bouncer" greeted the ladies and informed them they would be entering a men's club and, rules being rules, each woman would therefore need to don a fake moustache to pass muster for admittance. Amid giggles, the ladies eagerly complied and, one behind the other, made their way down the narrow stairs to the bar. The moustache moment invited the women to get ready for a bit of fun and helped them transition from tourist-businesswoman to underworld denizen about to playfully take a walk on the wild side, if only for an afternoon.

Within the bar's dark confines, a deejay played the thumping rhythm of club music as women were invited to a tongue-in-cheek immersion into the brand. Strolling in small groups from one artfully lighted part of the bar to the next, they saw demonstrations by Kiehl's skin- and hair-care specialists as they mixed and explained a variety of the company's most popular products. These mini hands-on workshops allowed the businesswomen to understand the essence of the product's formulation, ask the experts questions, and try a sample before the ring of a bell signaled it was time to move to the next mixologist's station.

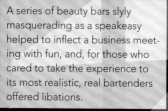
A series of beauty bars slyly
masquerading as a speakeasy
helped to inflect a business meeting with fun, and, for those who
cared to take the experience to
its most realistic, real bartenders
offered libations.

TAME THE BEAST

BOREDOM and excitement can never coexist in the same room. They're polar opposites, and they don't get along.

Excitement doesn't have to mean loud and splashy, though hallelujah for pumped-up music and fireworks! Excitement occurs when creativity comes to life. The only surefire way to avoid a boring event is to tap your inner creativity and bring it! Creativity kickstarts a party. It puts things in motion. And just when a lull threatens the mood, creativity shakes it up.

Unleashing that creativity gets a little tricky, however, when an honoree is so eccentric or a client's business is so abstract that finding a suitable theme for an event can fray your last creative nerve. Such was the case for a conference for people in the finance and investment community . . . who work in the global volatility market.

Ironically, for an industry centered on risk, events planned for this population rarely take one. Their meetings need to be on the serious side, without being dull. This is a crowd that sees gray suits every time they take an elevator. They deserve a lively event!

As we wrestled with a series of interlocking challenges—including dealing sensitively with a touchy subject and reaching the specific clientele—we devised a day that defined the conference with a standard so remarkable that the guests come back every year not because they need to, but because they want to.

We began by considering the nature of the business. In our first year, we took the letters V-O-L-A-T-I-L-I-T-Y and reproduced them as large three-dimensional sculptures. We placed them throughout the antechamber to the conference room in seemingly unsteady suspensions. The letter V was built from oversized playing cards stacked into a house—caught at the moment an ill wind began to blow it away. The O dangled above one side of a seesaw above dozens of eggs piled in a pyramid on the other side. The L appeared to be slipping on banana peels. Each letter became a metaphor that satisfied and teased.

Adding further dimension, actors portraying nineteenth-century paperboys hawked newspapers that blared headlines from major events in history, known in the trade as "tail events," that were game changers on the world financial stage.

Guests soon realized this was definitely not a typical business conference when, instead of a moderator imploring everyone to please take their seats, a high school marching band stomped loud and proud through the room with the band's "caboose" holding a banner that shouted, "Follow us to the presentation!" No one needed to be asked twice.

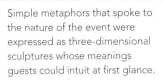

Simple metaphors that spoke to the nature of the event were expressed as three-dimensional sculptures whose meanings guests could intuit at first glance.

GLOBAL EDITION

A fascinating one day think tank bringing together the world's most progressive minds to debate, discuss, and offer fresh intelligence on volatility trading and volatility investing. Details, A2.

The Volatile Times

NEW YORK, 7 WORLD TRADE CENTER, MARCH 16, 2010

GLOBAL VOLATILITY SUMMIT 2010   FRE

TODAY'S AGENDA:
READ AT YOUR OWN RISK

MASS HYSTER

Unreliable S
to Be Expe

OFFICIALS
OF ANYT

GET AN
Genius

Got volatili
got answe
Genius
located
"geniu
throu
que
an
an

uriel Roubini:
lobal and U.S.
conomic Outlook

By Global Volatility

Council of Economic Advisors and then the Senior Advisor to the Under Secretary for International Affairs at the U.S. Treasury Department, helping to resolve the Asian and global financial crises amongst other issues. The International Monetary Fund, the World Bank and numerous other prominent public and private institutions have drawn upon his consulting expertise.

He has published over 70 theoretical, empirical and policy international published the

GLOBAL VOLATILITY SUMMIT 2010

8:00am - 9:00am	Breakfast
9:00am - 9:15am	Opening Remarks:
9:15am - 10:00am	KEYNOTE: Guest Speaker:
10:00am - 10:45am	PANEL 1: Panelists:

Paul Britton CEO / CRO, Capstone Investment Advisors, LLC

Global And US Economic Outlook – 2010
Nouriel Roubini Co-Founder and Chairman, Roubini Global Economics

Volatility Managers 2010 Outlook
Paul Britton CEO / CRO, Capstone Investment Advisors, LLC
Stephen Diggle Managing Partner, Artradis Fund Management
Alan Gerstein Senior Portfolio Manager, BlueMountain Capital Management
Geoffrey Duncombe Global Derivatives Strategist, Two Sigma Investments, LLC
Brett Barth Director of Investment Management/Founding Partner, BBR Partners

Moderator

Sponsored by NASDAQ

Acting Investment Manager, The Teacher

109

WHEN we were invited back for a second year in a row, the challenge had us knocking our heads against the wall. How could we make it work *twice*?

Our solution came in the form of visual reinterpretations of some of the most stunning "tail" events of modern times. We designed the Global Volatility Summit with the core of what the event was about: money. When creatively stumped, simply speak to the nature of the beast.

We wrapped the sponsor booths of the event in the currencies that sank or swam. One wall featured a super-sized $20 bill with bubble gum splattered across President Jackson's mug, a nod to the bursting of the American housing bubble in 2007. Dutch gilders served as fodder for a papier-mâché tulip beneath a bell jar, a visual retelling of the infamous speculative folly in tulip bulbs that nearly collapsed the world's economy in 1637. An Egyptian pound note caught former strongman Mubarak in the condemning gaze of Queen Nefertiti. *Sic semper tyrannis.*

As one of the most important and catastrophic events in recent memory, the bursting of the U.S. housing bubble received extra attention—with a dose of humor to instill a little levity into an otherwise quite serious conference.

GLOBAL
A THINK TANK BRINGING
TOGETHER DEBATE, DISCUSSION,
AND FRESH INTELLEGENCE

Entering guests were greeted by a large model ship—the *USS Global Volatility*—half-sunk into the floor, with huge plumes of baby's breath streaming from its smokestack.

In the guest lounge, visual metaphors serve as sculptural vignettes. The advent of the Great Depression is expressed literally, as the numbers in the year 1929 crash to the floor below, and a red zigzag in the carpet references the market's ups and downs.

Opposite: Sculptures revealing the conference's conceptual content serve not as decoration but as evocative art pieces that bear witness to centuries of "tail events," game-changing moments in history. A missing person notice on an enormous milk carton blares the disappearance of the Berlin Wall and the collapse of European Communism, while a three-dimensional line drawing captures the moment of the 1990s Dot-Com bust, and a sinking icon of a home bobs barely above the surface in a tank of mortgage debt.

A BIG TIME UNDER BIG TOP

IT's a common though incorrect assumption that to create a party space in your backyard, the simplest thing to do is to put up a tent. There's no space rental fee, after all, and the hours and catering and everything else are completely up to you. The inferred simplicity conceals what can become an incredibly complicated feat, with a myriad of minor obstacles to overcome. There is nothing inexpensive about a tent. A tented experience is actually among the most expensive types of events—when you erect a tent, you must fill the room inside from scratch.

Imagine building a large room in your backyard: you would need electricity, temperature control, a place for serving food and drinks, and a place to prepare food. A tent comes with all these same demands. Yet, nothing says "instant party here" quite like a tent. In a matter of hours, a lawn can suddenly sprout a room as elaborate as one at Versailles and the next day, barely a footprint remains.

Between the hours of setup and teardown, however, it takes a yeoman's labor—usually a team of yeoman—to get it right. And every step of the installation has to be designed and done in the proper sequence in order to pull the setup off without a hitch. Oh, so many potential hitches . . .

In short, a party in a tent requires the skills of an architect, engineer, set designer, scheduler, decorator, project manager, and dream-maker all in one. And that's all before the first mint julep is served.

If your outdoor space has special emotional importance, then a tent is worth every penny. After all, if the rolling pastures beyond your yard are also the place where your little girl played growing up, then what better spot for her wedding?

When we were asked to plan a wedding at a family's horse farm in upstate New York, we took one trip to the site and immediately understood their desire to stay close to home for the big day. Everywhere you looked—mountains, valleys, the landscaped grounds and the farm itself—the views were spectacular. Still, the setup required us to meet almost every challenge a tent experience brings, including dealing with a way to keep guests cool on a July afternoon. As anybody knows, a space that's too hot or cold is an instant party killer.

The outside ceremony and cocktail hour meant the blazing heat would kill our flowers very quickly, so we had to ensure that they—and all other perishables, including the wedding party's demeanor—stayed fresh until the six o'clock ceremony. What we normally accomplish in a full day of work in an indoor, air-conditioned space turned into a last-minute scramble. All boutonnières and arrangements had to be whisked into place looking crisp and cool, an effort that requires a small army acting as a well-oiled machine, pulling it together as if by magic. As if.

We turned the tent into a room that replicated the interior of the nearby farmhouse by covering the tent walls in the same wall-paper and adding finishes that concealed all evidence of the tent's utilitarian structure.

123

Clockwise from top left:
A handsome denizen of the horse farm keeps an eye on festivities. Crispy crackers cleverly shaped into rings and topped with tiny heaps of caviar jewels were created by caterer extraordinaire Peter Callahan. A bar set up on the lawn featured fresh cherries, a delicious, in-season alternative to bowls of mixed nuts, and pitchers of blackberry-cherry mojitos. A table offered pairs of flip-flops in bags specially printed with images of a horse and the wedding date. Ladies could switch to the comfy slip-ons while walking from cocktails on the lawn to the dinner tent and use the bag to hold their heels until arrival. Cocktails on the lawn offered a panoramic mountain view. Cool libations in mason jars await in the shade of a vase of simple Queen Anne's Lace.

After the ceremony, we lured our guests to the dinner party via a path lined with lanterns strewn across the lawn. As the guests approached the tent, the lights alongside grew in number and width so that at the final destination, the tent was surrounded by a sea of flickering lanterns, a glimmering cloud of luminaires floating around an island of festivity and joy.

Rustic-yet-formal touches such as wood-bead chandeliers, elegantly set tables lit with hurricane candles, and polished wood chairs create a space that is elegant but not overly fussy.

There are as many styles of tents as there are parties, but balancing the pros and cons of a tent and deciding whether it makes sense to even use one should be your first consideration—there's more to using this type of handy temporary event space than just propping up a canvas roof and taking it down at the end of the day. Keep in mind that a tent should solve more problems than it causes!

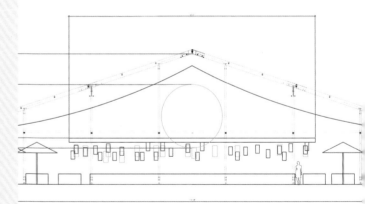

To tent or not to tent—that is the question.

Before you can decide if a tent is the right event choice, consider what a tent would bring to the party. The main purpose of a tent is to shield you from inclement weather—heat, cold, and especially rain. Unless the party is in a part of the world with very little chance of rain, every outdoor event needs a rain option. Tents provide a reliable alternative.

Pick a tent style that suits your event.

Tents, like events, come in all sizes, from tiny canopies the size of a carport to enormous stilted complexes that can house thousands of guests. Just as you would with any party space, match the room to the crowd. And don't forget style—would an old-fashioned circus tent; a Moroccan tent emblazoned with Moorish designs; or an extremely modern, clear-span tent with sleek straight lines, clear walls, a clear top, and no center poles enhance your theme best? And don't forget Old Reliable, the classic, real canvas tents made by a company called Sperry.

Choose a tent that suits the location.

If the event is in the middle of an enormous farm field, you can pick any tent that can be staked down. Tents designed for city rooftops, though, must be installed with external ballasts. Also remember that while tents with clear walls and ceilings look like glass, they are really just made of clear plastic and amplify inside temperatures under a bright sun. At night, there's no point to a clear tent . . . it will only make you feel like you're standing under a big, black garbage bag.

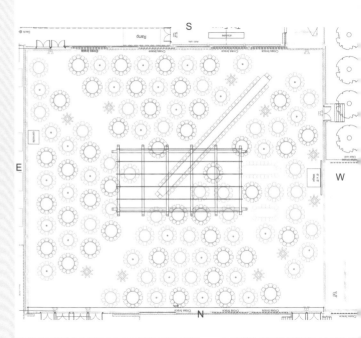

Work with a professional.

You wouldn't think of adding a room onto your house without calling on a professional—treat tents with equal respect. You need someone with the engineering know-how to understand weight issues, wind shear, permit requirements, and the local tenting codes. Even temporary structures are often subject to laws. The last person you want to show up at your party is a fire marshal or cop! They *will* issue tickets for breaking safety codes or noise restrictions. Tent companies will also serve as your guide on crucial issues such as restroom trailers, heating or cooling options, flooring, carpeting, safety railings, and so on.

BRACE yourselves: tent rental fees are not the biggest tenting expense! If you want anything besides a grass floor, you'll see labor and materials costs jump. The less level a property, the more costly the floor—you'll need to even out the ground or put in some sort of foundation. A flat walking surface makes it easy for guests to maneuver, and floors also keep feet dry in case of rain. No one wants to be known as the host who soaked everyone's Jimmy Choo suede shoes—*quelle horreur*! We've also learned to live by this directive: If you don't plan for rain, it surely will.

Flooring comes in a range of budget options; the advantages make the design choice worth pursuing. Portapath is a roll-out, modular plastic system that stands about an inch and half above the ground, and it can be covered in carpet or artificial grass. It follows the contours of the earth, though, so if the ground is sloped, your tent floor will, too. Portapath is best for covering flat but unsightly surfaces, such as parking lots or rooftops.

The next option is building up a wood foundation. If you are going to put carpet or artificial grass on over it, the tent company simply lays down inexpensive plywood and covers it. The most expensive option is to lay a beautiful hardwood floor. This gives you a sturdy foundation and flooring as elegant as any indoor party space can offer. But be sure you're sitting down when the installers present their cost estimate!

Raising the Roof

PARTIES AS THEATER

PARTIES are live theater, but the guests aren't there as audience, they're the heart of the performance, the actors themselves. This isn't about watching people on a stage. It's about being the people on the stage. And like theater, regardless of the money poured into the set, however excellent the script, no matter the reputation of the playwright, if the performers don't come through, if they don't believe and throw themselves into it wholeheartedly, the whole production falls flat. The guests need to commit. The host's role is to help them by investing thoughtfully in the party's look and feel.

For the *Huffington Post*'s annual 100 Game Changers party, the curtain came up the moment guests—many of whom *were* actual actors—arrived. The fête honors, in the words of the website's founder Arianna Huffington, "100 innovators, mavericks, visionaries, and leaders who are changing the world and the way we live in it." These up-and-coming movers and shakers and headline makers from entertainment, politics, sports, environmental organizations, education, media, style, tech, travel, business, and food would have been at home in any exclusive nightclub in Hollywood.

Yet this event became an *inclusive* club, one where the concept of celebrity went far deeper than the superficial notions usually associated with fame. Where else could you see, for example, Sean Penn hobnobbing with Anderson Cooper—not to discuss the Oscar-winning actor's latest film appearance, but his charity work in Haiti? Or Alyssa Milano, not there to publicize her role as the girl next door who charmed in *Charmed*, but as a member of the Twitterati whose innovative feed doesn't track her daily latte consumption, but instead raises thousands of dollars for important causes such as Charity Water?

Within the chosen party space, a white box of a gallery, we staged a production as multifaceted as the personalities the event honored while also telegraphing the high-spirited pop and glamour of a big-celebrity party—a deep, entrancing, welcoming event with the occasional plot twist, like a good play.

The event's design aimed to honor each profession with a décor that also created a compelling visual exhibition, akin to the party's mise-en-scène. This night was meant to take stock of some of the world's hottest and most cutting-edge personalities. So we sought a décor that combined plenty of style, but with meaning behind the glitz.

Large welded steel-wire constructions, painted and lit in bright fluorescent colors, became etched two- and three-dimensional sculptures suspended overhead or displayed on plinths, each a tip of the hat to an honoree's professional discipline. The sculptural optical illusions echoed the quasi-physicality of cyberspace entities such as the *Huffington Post*—though it exists solely as an intangible, it has nonetheless proved to be a very substantial force in the world.

The evening's look was a stroke of stagecraft that created theater in the round, where the guests could play out their public roles of being honored in literal and metaphorical midstride. It also removed the usual formality associated with awards ceremonies so everyone could just enjoy the party. Using lighting, sets, furniture, and flow, we prodded the drama forward with a verve and spirit that was as alive and vibrant as each honoree.

Sculptural neon displays announce award categories—fashion, technology, food, sports, politics. The result is a décor as edgy as the community and the dialogue the *Huff Post* fosters.

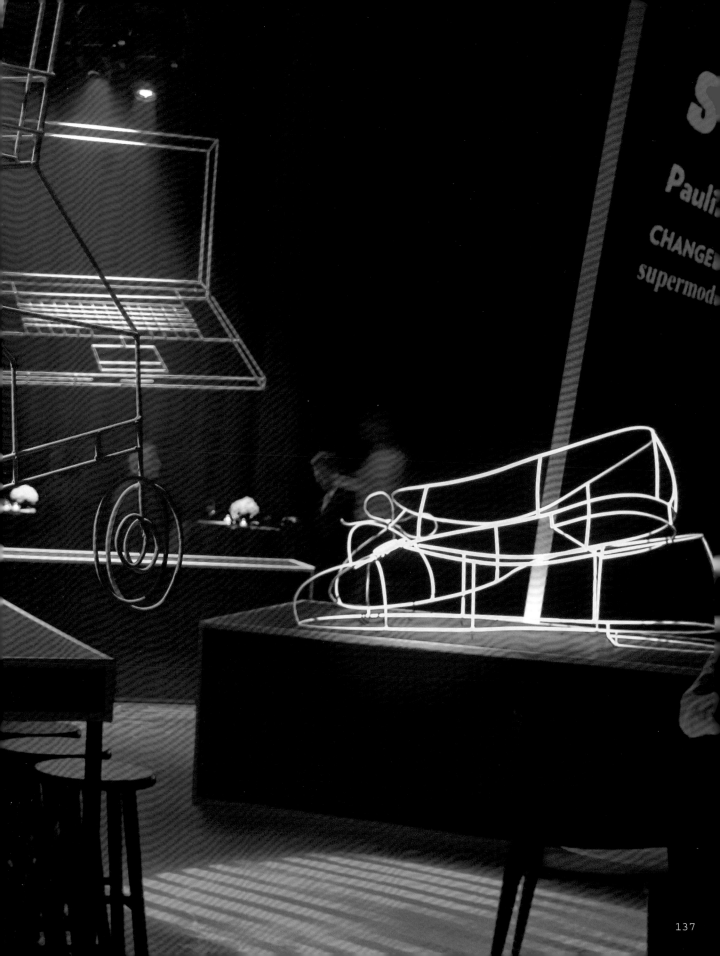

The setting helped to create an atmosphere of one big, sexy cocktail party where the guests—regardless of fame or stature—could lounge comfortably and be at once seen and not seen in a space that was part gallery, part club, but 100 percent interactive theater.

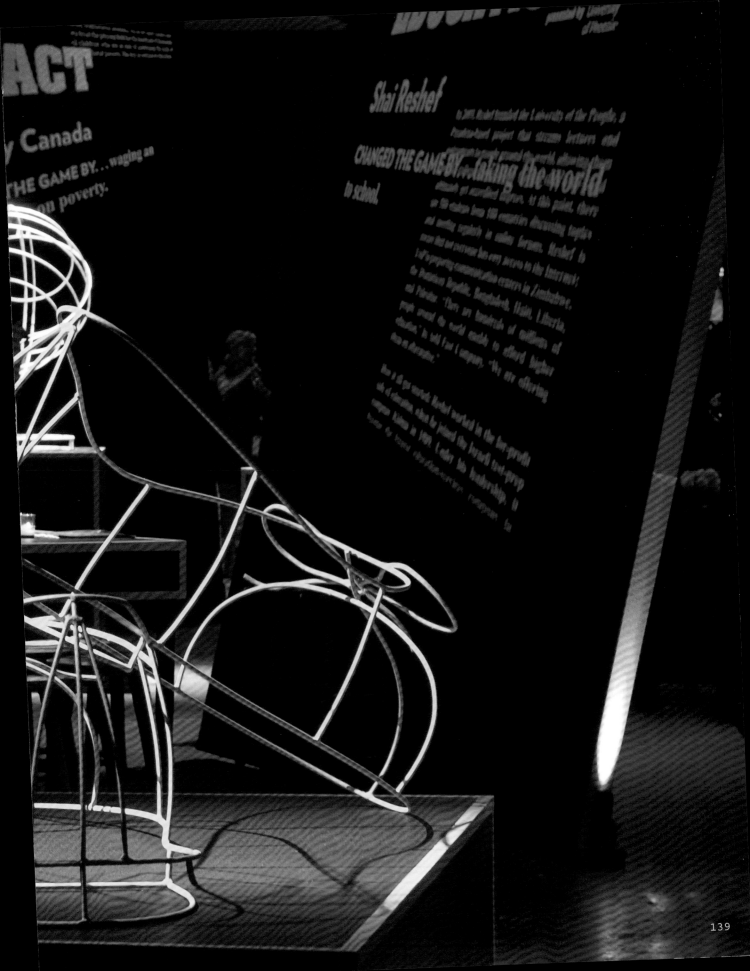

During the evening, various speakers approached a podium at the front of the event space to speak briefly about each honoree. Here, in a room full of completely different personalities, the lights came up on a new kind of star—intent not on fame but on making real-world differences.

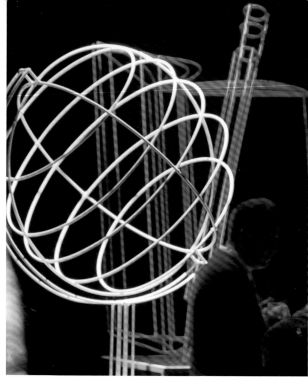

THE BIG PICTURE

THE Museum of Contemporary Art, North Miami is the little engine that could. Inaugurated in 1996, what started out as a local arts organization with a small collection has blossomed into a world-class cultural institution. In that time, the museum has celebrated collaborations with the Tate Modern in London, the Los Angeles Museum of Contemporary Art, and the Metropolitan Museum in New York, and featured a stellar range of artists including Ed Ruscha, Jorge Pardo, and Matthew Barney. But it never took time to celebrate itself.

It finally decided to throw a birthday party on its fifteenth anniversary. This party had to cover all the bases required of any nonprofit's fund-raiser and also serve as a coming-out party for one knockout of a deb. This would be an introduction to the larger world that extolled the past, marked the present, and generated excitement for the future.

If you take a conceptual approach, you can often imbue otherwise mundane components of an event with meaning. If the look relates to what's happening, then the look has meaning. The superficial becomes profound.

We began by camping out in the museum's archives and plowing through their records of every exhibit, acquisition, press clipping, promotional flyer, and event. Then, somewhere between rifling through old catalogs and reviewing invitation designs, it struck us. For this first big party, we could literally take a page—in fact, many thousands of pages—from MOCA's brief but bright history.

If you understand the big picture, you can paint the big picture.

With a guest list of six hundred, we planned a cocktail hour followed by dinner followed by entertainment. First we cleared out every piece of art from the museum's galleries, which served as our party space. We then took all our collected ephemera—either excess materials from the archives or copies we made—sized them into 6-inch squares, and divided them into stacks of primary and secondary colors.

We wallpapered the walls from floor to ceiling with a grid of colors, wrapping each room in a progressive rainbow and turning the museum itself into an art installation. The entire dinner walked the line between the literal and the abstract—a fitting balance for an institution dedicated to modern art—and coalesced these two very different narratives into a cohesive presentation. From a distance, a vibrant color wheel; up close, the literal story of the museum.

Standard centerpieces and soft candlelight would have come up short. Aligning our design agenda with the very essence of the museum itself created an emotional investment for the guest, a moment in time to last beyond a moment. When decoration has meaning, it helps guests relate. But this went beyond decoration—it was heart and soul. It had depth, meaning, and a message with lasting power. It's like the difference between Aretha and a pop star of the moment: when something's got soul, you can feel it.

an Lehman

useum of Contemporary Art

MUSEUM OF
CONTEMPORARY ART
NORTH MIAMI

The walls, papered with a grid of vibrant images drawn directly from the museum's own archives, and the tables, topped with acrylic triangles that enclosed open-faced exhibit catalogs turned objects *about* art into objects *of* art.

Countless catalogs, former show announcements, posters, invitations, press items, and other printed ephemera from the museum's archives were refashioned into uniform six-inch squares, creating a design building block we pieced together into an orchestrated chaos that delivered swaths of design from a distance and tantalizing bites of history upon closer inspection.

MO
CA

MO
CA
MUSEUM OF CONTEMPORARY ART

an Lehman Building
70 NE 125th St.
orth Miami, Fl 33161

roceeds will benefit
MOCA's Permanent
ollection Acquisition Fund
nd Programming. To find
ut more information, please
g onto our website at
www.mocanomi.org
call 305.893.6211

The simple, effective scheme of repurposed paper also played out in voluminous drum shades—with woven diamond shapes that continued the color grid of ephemera.

MO
CA

15TH ANNIVERSARY

FIRST COURSE
WARM WATERCRESS SOUP
FLOATING 'ISLAND' SAVORY CHOUX PASTRY
AMERICAN CAVIAR, CRÉME FRAICHE, PATE AUX CHOUX

MAIN COURSE
WHOLE ROASTED AND SLICED SIRLOIN OF BEEF
RED WINE SAUCE, CRISPY LEEKS
PURPLE MASHED POTATOES, BEET ROOT OIL
SPINACH PURSES

DESSERT
MOCA GEOMETRICS
RECTANGLE – TWO-STAGE BITTERSWEET VALHRONA CHOCOLATE TORTE
SPHERE – VANILLA-SCENTED HOMEMADE FROMAGE BLANC
ROD – HAZELNUT + ALMOND MERINGUE
STAR – RED RASPBERRY GELEE
CARAMEL + ESPRESSO SAUCES

WINE
PROVIDED BY DUCKHORN
2010 MIGRATION RUSSIAN RIVER CHARDONNAY
2009 DUCKHORN VINEYARDS NAPA VALLEY MERLOT

VEGETARIAN OPTION AVAILABLE

As part of the evening's festivities, fun performance artist Ragnar Kjartansson cast his spell with a jaw-dropping aria starring show-girls decked head to toe in feathers and sequins that exploded in a climax of cannons shooting bombs of confetti over the crowd.

SOME party themes are so rich, so varied, and so versatile they practically beg to be reincarnated again and again. And when a theme is good, it will not only repeatedly pass the "intrigue" test with flying colors, it will soar.

As master architect Eero Saarinen noted when he created his monumental arch in St. Louis, relying on a classic shape—an arch, a dome, a cube—gives you an automatic design advantage since you needn't convince anyone to like it. Party themes follow a similar trajectory. Employ a classic theme and you already have an appealing start. From there it's only a matter of embellishing it with your imagination.

Books hold this kind of design promise. Books can "literally" take you anywhere— and often to places you never imagined. This metaphor and the magic between the covers of classic books directly translate to event design excitement potential—think about bringing Dorothy's Kansas to life or and letting Alice look on the other side of the glass. Books are a very simple object with a quite profound range.

We've created several parties centered on books, yet each design was Dewey decimals apart from the other. Keeping each party original despite simultaneously relying on a similar theme is akin to an artist returning to a favorite subject— think Monet and his lilies or Picasso and Dora Maar—the theme may be revisited, but each canvas stands as a unique work of art and, with the right touch, a potential masterpiece. It's the difference between an original work of art and a paint-by-number copy. Pick a theme that means something important to you, and use that theme as a conduit for creativity.

Any common object can be the starting point for any number of parties. The gatherings can be as varied in purpose as a rocking bat mitzvah or a sophisticated afternoon luncheon for a coterie of successful businesswomen, but they can all use the same object in slightly different ways. We started with the simple but powerful premise that, just as the stories within books can take you anywhere, a design theme as versatile as books can take you anywhere, too. There are as many ways to craft that theme as there are types of books themselves.

For our bat mitzvah, for example, we started with the guest of honor's love of Harry Potter. Like millions of other 13-year-olds around the world, she had spent a considerable amount of time poring through the world of Harry and his compatriots at Hogwarts. There's nothing new about using Harry Potter as a party theme—but we decided to take what could easily turn into a pastiche of childish touchstones (imagine a Harry lookalike arriving mid-party in full wizard drag) and refashioned it in a way that spoke to the meaning of the milestone itself.

The essence of a bat mitzvah, of course, celebrates the fact that the little girl that was is no longer. Yet, at thirteen, she's still very young. So we had to find that sweet spot between those two stages in life with a theme that comfortably fit those two worlds, and, just as J.K. Rowling's masterful writing has done—find cool and avoid cheeseball. So as we approached our design, we kept in mind that this party setting was not about the "magic" of Harry Potter, but the magic of reading. And we never forgot that just as books are a journey, so too is a party. The answer came in the form of a sit-down dinner held amid a massive, oversized "library" filled with the hostess's literary favorites and the look and feel of books, books, books everywhere.

A book-centric invitation crafted by Cheree Berry set the party's theme in motion.

NO. 2012

The celebration continues immediately following
583 Park Avenue
Park Avenue
at East Sixty-third Street

DUE	NAME	RETURNED
01/07/12	C.S.	

RSVP

44

stamps.com

512 FIFTH AVENUE · APARTMENT 5B · NEW YORK, NY 10075

CS

're invited
to a
vel affair...

PARTY OF THE YEAR
CS
JANUARY SEVENTH, 2012

THE CANDYMAKERS

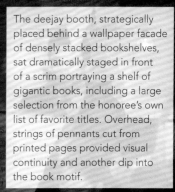

The deejay booth, strategically placed behind a wallpaper facade of densely stacked bookshelves, sat dramatically staged in front of a scrim portraying a shelf of gigantic books, including a large selection from the honoree's own list of favorite titles. Overhead, strings of pennants cut from printed pages provided visual continuity and another dip into the book motif.

Dinner tables sported rows of books as centerpieces, interrupted by vases disguised as stacks of books. Each floral arrangement sprouted vivid mixes of ranunculus, tulips, and daffodils. Books on tall stems held each table's number aloft, the numerals themselves cut from more pages of print.

AT another point further along the age spectrum, a sixtieth birthday for a successful businesswoman also provided a fitting venue for a theme about books, though with a totally fresh point of view. "Everyone's lives are filled with stories," read a huge, open book placed at the front of the luncheon, held in the lobby of a theater in Washington, D.C., where the birthday gal has had a long commitment to the local arts scene. "You are an important part of mine."

This simple, yet poignant, message offered two grand opportunities. The notion of stories let us design a party around the vibrancy of storytelling and the power of books. At the same time, it let the party guests know how much they meant to the hostess—the open book was like the hostess herself spreading her arms wide in enthusiastic welcome— and how this event was less about honoring her than them. That type of generosity brings up a good rule of thumb for all parties: make the party about your guests. Make it something special for them, a brief passage of time filled with joy and friendship that may possibly bring them years of wonderful memories.

A one-two punch of the grand and the intimate gives a party substance. You want a wow factor the moment your guests arrive. This oversized book's welcoming message saw to that!

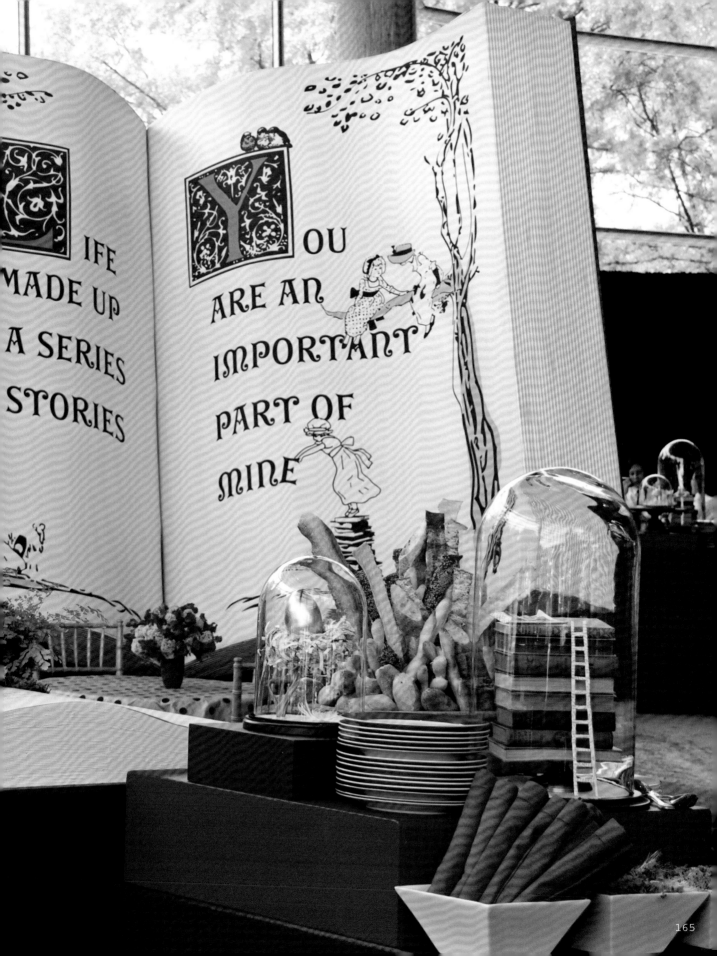

To give the eye plenty to linger over, we created a series of small, thematic visual treats. A paper castle crafted from book pages and placed atop a green mountain of moss festooned the salad station, a large paper bonsai tree cut from an oversized printed page anchored a spread with an Asian-fusion flare, and bell jars at the various stations held tiny treasures—like a petite fairy with paper wings and a paper pearl tucked inside a real oyster shell at the seafood station.

arly for the
walked about and looked at
ned animals, which they had
Little Reader, have
monkeys,
great

Color names drawn from Benjamin Moore's newest line, Color Stories, metaphorically become books whose spines reflect their true hues.

BOOKS again became the reference—pun intended—when Benjamin Moore asked us to dream up its entry for the annual DIFFA fund-raiser, Dining by Design, a showcase that raises money to directly benefit those living with HIV/AIDS and for education outreach to at-risk communities. With the company's spectacular new line of paint, Color Stories, as our guiding force, we constructed a dining room that could only be entered through an opening within a row of giant books.

Once inside, we let the color spectrum whisk visitors away on a feast of fantasy. The table, made up of nothing but books from legs to top, featured a swarm of paper butterflies. In a panorama of hues plucked straight from the rainbow—this was, after all, a paint company's showroom—the little creatures flitted and flew above the books.

Open books across each table setting featured paper pop-ups bespeaking the possibilities of where the realm of reading can take us, a delicious metaphor indeed. Even though we relied on the theme of books again, we let it take us to a place where we had never been before, just like a brand new story from a favorite author.

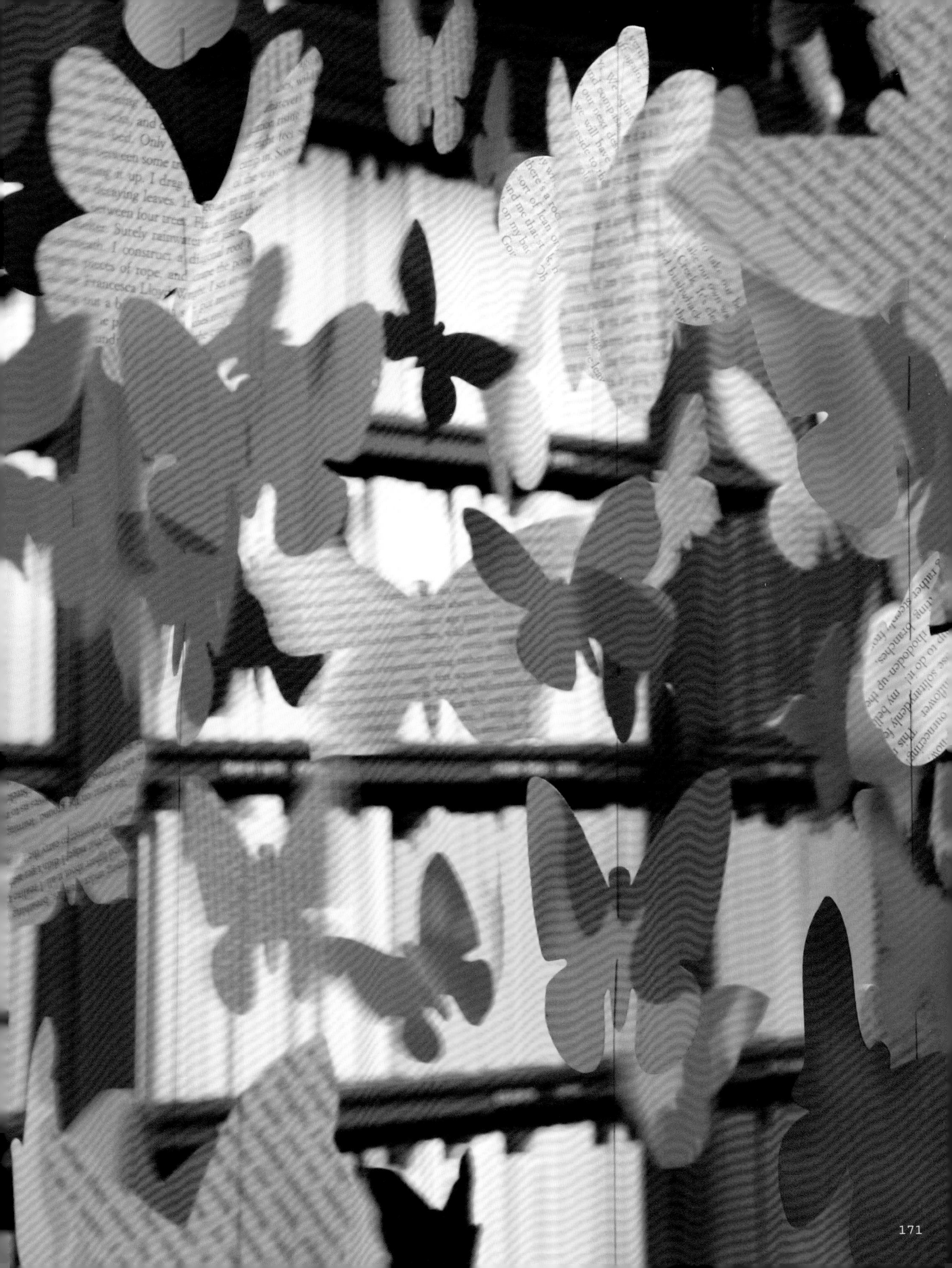

hannah banana CSP-955   goldsmith CSP-960

walk on the beach CSP-975   honeybee CSP-950

GOLDEN
FIELDS

golden thread CSP-920

The same brilliant gold woven through the gold
colored Balinese wedding suit. Imagine it
swirling through the warm, candlelit night

FIERY SUNSET

sheer bliss CSP-545

VIOLET
TWILIGHT

waterloo CSP-555   purplicious CSP-465

daydream CSP-615

pressed violet CSP-520   fancy pants CSP-58

FLUID BLUES

antique glass CSP-695

in the tropics CSP-640

berry fizz
CSP-4

raspberry glaze
CSP-450

Guests stepped through a row
of oversized book spines into
a world of color, not unlike
Dorothy stepping from Kansas
into a Technicolor Oz. Inside, an
array of charming paper cutouts
including marching brass bands,
autumn leaves, an artist at his
easel, and a rainbow of butterflies
in flight rise directly from the
pages of open books.

SHADES OF GRAY

OL 2 NATURALLY NEUTRAL

VOL 3 EARTHEN HUES

VOL 4 VIOLET TWILIGHT

VOL 5 FLUID BLUES

VOL 6 ELEMENTAL GREENS

VOL 7 GOLDEN FIELDS

VOL 8 FIERY SUNSET

Benj

MARTINI OLIVE

INGENUITY IN THE HOUSE

EVERY party has a budget. It may be a number followed by several zeroes or just a couple of crisp twenties, but there will always be a set amount to be spent. The critical factor with money—like time—is how you spend it. No matter how tight your finances, you can always afford to make a fun event. Budgets shouldn't limit you—never approach a party with an attitude that the design must be commensurate with budget. Remember that it's only the dollar amount that is limited, not your imagination.

Even with a sky-high amount of money to spend, the goal should be to evoke awe and amazement at the setting for the setting's sake, not to have people think "Oh, my, how expensive all this must have been."

Approach a budget as a reality to master rather than a constraint. If, as a bride, you can't afford a big bouquet, pick one gorgeous, exquisite flower—a massive peony, perhaps, or a stunning rose—and tie it in a satin bow. If the chairs available at a venue have four legs, those legs reach the floor, and you can make them work with your design, consider that good enough and don't blow cash on renting others. Best your budget, don't kowtow to it.

An annual New Yorkers for Children fund-raiser, a spring dance dubbed the "Fool's Fête," raises money and awareness for a good cause, but it still needs a fresh approach each year. For a charity function, the last thing someone should think when entering the room is, "So . . . my donation is going to pay for pricey doodads." I just want them to think, "Wow!"

Our solution? After landing on a theme of the sublimities of India, we began by sending vellum paper through photocopiers to mass-produce a print of distinctly smart paisleys. We pressed that irrepressible pattern into service as a design mainstay on tear-shaped surrounds for our tabletop votives. Along with spindly mandalas, rakish peacocks, and other imagery, our designs conjured the exoticism of the subcontinent using bare-bones, black-and-white line drawings softened by the vellum, an inexpensive choice of materials, and artful placement around (again, inexpensive) votives and pillar candles of various heights that brought in drama on a dime.

We also made photocopies of hands decorated in henna as our table numbers, a design choice as effective in visual power as it was in fiscal austerity. Call it party by photocopy. Yet there was nothing low-rent about our money-saving tactics; our focus remained intent on demonstrating what we really *could* do with only a dollar, not what we *couldn't* do with only a dollar.

Perhaps you could buy the basic ingredients and throw an ice-cream-and-lemonade social in the shade of your back porch—extra points for a hand-cranked ice cream machine where everyone takes a turn crafting the main course. Or budget for mixers and throw a BYOB-slash-BYOV—a bring-your-own-beverage/bring-your-own-vinyl affair. Then push back the furniture and make room for an evening of kicking it old school. *Disco Inferno!*

Paisleys—those curved, feathery forms that made a splash in 1960s America along with gurus, Nehru jackets, and all things sitar—have had great staying power and still work well as a decorative motif today.

179

179

Saffron, vermilion, and gold vellum curled into slender tubes, held simply with double-stick tape to make happy diamond shapes, and lined up in a circle around table lights atop tall, slender poles create hand-crafted chandeliers that drench the room with a golden hue.

WHEN we scout sites for a party, we're like real estate agents, mixing the needs and budget of the client with a search list of potential spots that fit the bill. Most of all, what we look for is a place that feels just right, where the host, guests, and theme will all feel cozy—at home, if you will.

Beyond budget, part of the reason a space works for an event is its location—literally where it sits on the map. Can people get there easily? Is transportation a problem or is it hard to find? Then there are the physical realities of the space. Is it accessible to the physically challenged? Can it hold all the guests you want to invite? Can it host a dinner, cocktail hour, dancing, a band?

Some event spaces are obviously right and, often, obviously wrong. You wouldn't, for example, hold a bar or bat mitzvah in a church reception hall. If the setting is a barn filled with hay bales, you might enjoy a barbecue—perhaps even a sit-down rustic dinner—but the folksy setting would run contrary, say, to a party with a digital or futuristic theme. That's not to say you can't go for surprise, such as a party at the Plaza that revels in downtown street culture and derives energy from juxtaposition. But it's a careful balance. Finally, when on a real estate scouting expedition, there's the all-important but oh-so-elusive "vibe." When you enter the space do you have that inimitable feel that this is *the* place?

We knew we had hit the mark when we peeked our heads into the Milstein Hall of Ocean Life at New York's American Museum of Natural History—it was perfect for a fund-raiser benefitting the Natural Resources Defense Council. Both museum and council share a dedication to understanding and protecting the environment and all the creatures of the earth—including the two-legged species invited to the evening's event.

The signature emblem of the museum's grand hall is a life-sized replica of a blue whale suspended from the ceiling. As anyone who has looked up at this magnificent sculpture knows, it's so real you can imagine being in scuba gear as one of the gargantuan denizens of the deep swims overhead. It's phenomenal. The room is a popular spot for all kinds of events, from weddings to corporate parties, but it's often treated as if it were any other reception hall. This is worse than ignoring the proverbial elephant in the room—in this case even a large pachyderm (with all due respect) would be small peanuts—it's ignoring the largest animal on the planet *that's floating right over your head!*

We embraced the mighty leviathan as our event's unofficial mascot, an awesome symbol of the valiant goals of the council and its members. To give the event soul, to bring its message home for the invited guests, we developed a theme for the evening in conjunction with the NRDC that would serve as an adjunct to the whale, landing upon "What are you a part of?" The theme tapped each individual's contribution to the organization and the planet and, at the same time, underscored the tight community ties among the council's membership.

IF THE SITE FITS

...aths Best Defense

NEW YORK, MONDAY, NOVEMBER 14, 2011

Voters Support Clean Energy and Climate Solutions

NRDC will continue to push lawmakers to pass clean energy and climate policies

By PETER LEHNER
Executive Director, Natural Resources Defense Council

Gas Mileage Gains Move the Country Forward

By PETER LEHNER
Executive Director, Natural Resources Defense Council

Meet the Change Makers
Steering Ford Toward Sustainability

By ADAM ASTON

Sparking Inspiration and Fueling Our Clean Technology Economy
PAGE 4

Obama Presents NRDC Founder John Adams with a Presidential Medal of Freedom

By FRANCES BEINECKE, President, Natural Resources Defense Council

> "the Presidential Medal of Freedom, the highest civilian honor in the United States."

Putting a Lid on America's Trash Trail

By KATHERINE BAGLEY

NRDC
THE EARTH'S BEST DEFENSE

Let's Develop Wind, and Other Cleaner, More Sustainable Sources of Power and Fuel

By ROBERT REDFORD
Actor, Director, Environmental...

Let's invest in high-speed rail, smart communi...

Scientific Study Links Flammable Drinking Water to Fracking

By ABRAHAM LUSTGA...

EXPLORE NRDC VICTORIES 1971
NRDC wins passage of the Clean Water Act, which allows citizens to sue polluters directly. PAGE 9

EXPLORE NRDC VICTORIES 1978
NRDC wins fight to remove ozone depleting CFCs from aerosol cans. PAGE 5

EXPLORE NRDC VICTORIES 1985
NRDC helps win adoption of national efficiency standards for consumer appliances, saving billions of dollars on electrical bills. PAGE 8

EXPLORE NRDC VICTORIES 1992
NRDC helps stop New York City's practice of dumping processed sewage in the ocean, eliminating the practice in the United States altogether. PAGE 6

EXPLORE NRDC VICTORIES 2001
NRDC's decade-long campaign to reduce arsenic in drinking water calls on the EPA adopting stricter arsenic in water treatment. PAGE 6

EXPLORE NRDC VICTORIES 2007
NRDC, and our partners win a historic Supreme Court ruling that global warming emissions are "pollutants" under the Clean Air Act and that the EPA has authority to curb those pollutants. PAGE 7

EXPLORE NRDC VICTORIES 2010
In a major court victory in 2010, halted plans to drill in millions spanning Alaska's Chukchi Sea, United States two "Polar Bear Seas"

ACTION CENTER
19
WHO WE ARE

We constructed large facsimiles of newspapers with headlines that shouted out the NRDC's successes and replaced the photo spaces with natural and environmentally minded images to make a backdrop that added to the event's dynamism and theme.

Each seating area featured mini tableaux that highlighted delicate specimens from nature—a single blossom, a sea urchin—under bell jars, often with magnifying glasses nearby to help guests inspect the contents closely. We also created sculptures of animals from recycled electronics, such as a spindly daddy longlegs built from wire and keyboard keys. Both focused the evening on the cause at hand, but without being heavy-handed about it.

If ever there was a party where the needs of the guests drove the menu, it was this one. We eschewed serving any fish, fowl, or four-legged beast—consider the cause—and organized a vegetarian feast instead.

Think of party food as delicious décor. Like every other major element of an event, the food needs to fit with the overall theme. The food should be satisfying, nicely presented, and fit well with all of the main event's constraints, including budget, time, and space. It should serve as the event's most sensory component, but it also offers an opportunity to loop in another layer of meaning and nuance.

Make the meal fit the occasion. You can bet that an annual Natural Resources Defense Council benefit will have more than a few vegetarians in attendance, for example. Plan accordingly. And never let the meal work against the evening's theme. No Wiener schnitzel at a Tuscan-themed party. No messy make-your-own-tacos—no matter how local, organic, or gourmet the components—at a formal function.

Don't try to do too much. Nobody comes to an event of the food alone, and nobody expects four-star restaurant food at a party. It's great if it can be tasty, but it's always secondary. If it's free and it's on offer, they will eat it. Save yourself the headache of food gymnastics or any other service contortions that burden you with unnecessary worry—they usually leave guests unsatisfied or just plain confused anyway. Event food service is a science, but it doesn't need to be the Manhattan Project.

Limiting meal options is actually a courtesy. When you have a dinner party at home, you don't plan a menu with a wide array of choices, and neither should your event. Besides adding cost, too many food options are more time consuming for a waiter to jot down and the kitchen to cook and plate. The nicest thing you can do for guests is to feed them quickly and efficiently.

Favor foods suitable for catering, such as broiled or grilled meats or main courses that come from the oven and can be prepared largely in advance before the event begins. Even in a restaurant, after all, the chef doesn't throw together an individual pan of lasagna each time it's ordered. Remember that most caterers are working out of what are essentially glorified camp kitchens. If you as a client demand that they pan sauté, fry, or bake soufflés to order, they will probably give it their best shot, but if the effort (perhaps literally) falls flat, it's your failure, not theirs.

People don't come to a party hoping to have the best meal of their lives—the *time* of their lives, possibly! But food is only one component of the whole experience, and guests are realistic enough to know that quality must inevitably be sacrificed a little to quantity. Your decisions as host, though, can make or break a successful service.

Keep in mind that it's impossible to deliver either two dozen or 1,000 meals at once. Help the staff streamline the process by getting people to sit quickly and quit socializing when the appointed time for dinner arrives so that everyone can eat in a timely manner—before the chicken turns to rubber. Caterers perform simply amazing feats under difficult circumstances, but you ignore the reality of the kitchen's limitations at your peril. A good way to cue guests it's time to take their seats includes having the host rise and offer a brief welcome. If guests enter the dining area to a lively band, quiet the band down when it's time to sit—a cue that works unfailingly.

Don't forget the vegetarians! You don't have to announce a vegetarian plate as an option, but should any guest make that request, the kitchen should be able to offer a meal on par with the other main courses. Plan for up to 20 percent of diners to ask for it. A wonderful vegetarian plate fits in with what should always be the number-one goal of the meal and the event: the happiness of *all* your guests.

The
Party
on the
Plate

SOMETHING NEW UNDER THE SUN

A successful event reflects the host or hostess's personality. That means that when designing a bar mitzvah, we first sit down with the guest of honor to find out who he is, his likes, his cherished memories, and his hopes for the future. Due diligence sets a mundane event apart a from a memorable one. But, in the case of thirteen-year-olds, the inevitable answer to those probing questions—the result of our investigations to know precisely *what makes one tick*—often boils down to three simple words: "I like sports."

From Miami to Anchorage, boarding schooled or home-schooled, urban, suburban, or exurban, our in-depth social research reveals that boys on the cusp of manhood obsess about sports. We're committed to creating something unique with every event we design, so we constantly face a challenge of turning a basic, potentially run-of-the-mill theme into something we've never done before and that a client—and his guests, who will likely be attending a dozen or more bat and bar mitzvahs during the same year—has never experienced before.

And it can't just be a variation on a theme, a slight twist from what happened before. It has to be really different. These are young teens. They don't do nuance. And they'll call out something as boring in an instant.

One young New Yorker revealed a love for the Mets. It was our first inkling that we were working with someone special, a kid who would side with perennial underdogs over their cross-river rivals. A little more probing led us to discover his favorite color was hot pink! The mix of a typical boy and atypical panache created fire, which became our entrée to design a party that told an age-old theme in a brand new way.

The design relied on personal touches that translated to outsized punch, including creating a huge wall emblazoned with his name. The letters were made out of thousands and thousands of baseball cards he had collected. Other walls showed scrolling scenes of sporting moments, including snapshots of the young man on the fields of the several sports he plays. The hot pink gave us license to glow in the party's accents. Though not a hue normally associated with a sports-loving boy, it and other fluorescents are quite popular in skateboarding, extreme sports, and other high-octane activities—so it invited us to use a cutting-edge color template.

Any number of themes can veer toward the tedious and trite if not completely explored. A Hawaiian theme? Not again! But a journey into the erupting depths of Kilauea—now that's fresh. A beach theme? Oh, please! But an afternoon at Coney Island, complete with live sideshows, a beer garden and a henna tattoo parlor—now that sounds like a party. You have a lot of personality. So should your party.

The wall behind the service bar was covered end to end and top to bottom with baseball bats, while the front of the bar was decked out in collector's boxes of baseballs. Small signs on the bar let the guests know that all the equipment would later be donated to local sports teams chosen by the honoree—clearly a 13-year-old on his way to becoming not only a man, but a mensch

Thousands of baseball cards from the bar mitzvah's personal collection were pressed into service as decoration while a trio of seats rescued from Shea Stadium became an unconventional guest book. Stop-motion, three-dimensional illusions of various sports balls frozen in flight as they "bounced" from one tabletop to another injected a fitting dose of adrenaline.

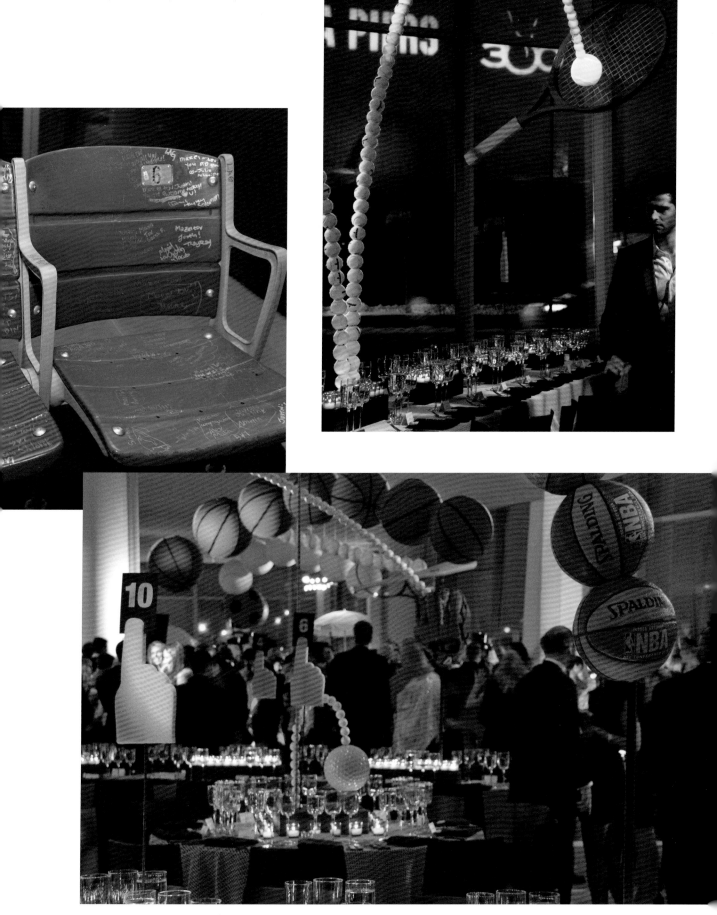

WHEREVER you create a party—regardless how large or small, whether a quiet cocktail reception or a mega-blowout—try to transform the space, to turn it from a location into a sensation. You can't move the walls, floor, or ceiling, but everything within that space is effectively potential energy. Just like you keep the look of your home—a place you've seen countless times before—fresh and interesting, make an event space look brand-new even if it's someplace you've seen countless times before. There's also a good chance your guests will have been to any given party space more than once in their lives, whether it's a rented banquet hall or the host's home, and probably more than once that year.

A transformed space gives a party its spark. It surprises even the most jaded of guests. And it tickles the event with youthful glee. "Old deeds for old people," as Thoreau once said, "and new deeds for new." Keep in mind that everybody, regardless of chronological age, wants to feel young and exuberant at a party.

Offer an idea that runs contrary to what's typically done—if you dare deviate from placing the stage or the band in the place where it normally pops up or if you advocate for something other than the standard "round tops in straight rows"—expect to run into a brick wall of opposition. There are countless reasons not to rock the boat. "We've always done it that way," says management. For any self-respecting event designer these words are akin to a line in the sand, and I'm precisely the type of person who must cross it.

Remember Arthur C. Clarke's description of the three-stage response to any new idea: "It can't be done." "It can be done, but it's not worth it." "What a great idea!" A sharp focus on newness, on developing unique designs and brand-new themes, sets a tone that keeps a party fresh and encourages guests to take the plunge and enjoy themselves.

For an example of how to do this—and a space that understands the need to keep things fresh—I offer as Exhibit A the amazing Cipriani's, New York's Forty-Second Street party temple that was once the grand lobby of a nineteenth-century bank. Its soaring ceilings and dramatic details ooze elegance. It's also home to dozens of events on the social calendar, so whether it's the first time or the fiftieth time a guest enters that room, they need to feel as though they are experiencing something new.

For the hundredth anniversary of *Women's Wear Daily*, we sifted through the thousands of covers the venerated journal has produced over the past century and came up with a wall papered in a montage of images worthy of Warhol. It was a version of the "step and repeat" wall, where arriving guests are photographed against a backdrop that artfully repeats the client's name and logo so that no matter how the photo is later cropped, you can always see it. For purposes of the party, the wall literally tells guests, "You've arrived!" At the same time, it gives a preview of the excitement behind the wall without revealing too much. Everyone likes a little tease, right?

We let the fantastic graphics of the magazine itself be our main inspiration. The concept was elegant, intriguing, and evocative, just like a juicy *WWD* cover story. We made umbrellas from the pages of *WWD* and dangled cascading strings of crystal raindrops from inside. We built an enormous birthday cake upon hundreds of issues of *WWD*. We reconstructed the workspace of an imagined *WWD* reporter that featured all the accoutrements of the journalist's life, including a live desktop I-Mac scrolling through images of iconic fashions and a vase of freshly-sharpened #2 Ticonderogas.

We dressed mannequins in dazzling fashions from the houses of today's most important designers, which were auctioned for charity later in the evening. We even outfitted one model with a stack of gift-wrapped goodies that towered up into the eaves, nearly reaching the top of Cipriani's high ceiling. Around the room, we flashed an ever-changing array of fashion photography on a series of large screens, drenching the space in color and light. Besides creating visual interest, these vignettes also served as conversational focal points and icebreakers.

This room's classic lines and baroque styling allow it to sport a variety of looks, in the same way a museum's galleries can display art ranging from ancient Sumerian treasures to an installation by Richard Serra.

Keep in mind that guests come and go throughout the evening. Thus, a guest list totaling seven hundred translates into a substantially smaller crowd at any given moment. Since this was a cocktail party, that meant we could do away with tables and the need to have a chair for every guest. A good rule is to have enough chairs for 20 percent of the guests expected at any one time.

Past issues of *WWD* themselves became the inspiration—and literal foundation—for the design details that peppered the space.

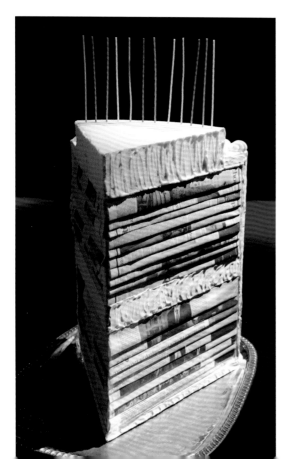

The strict monetary limitations imposed by the nonprofit host's budget were put to the test by the schedule for the evening, which called for a cocktail party for five hundred, followed by a seated dinner, and an awards show and entertainment. Here, simple rolls of colorful ribbon fit the literal bill, and helped us transform the space by giving it a dimensionality none of the guests had ever experienced before.

WHEN it came time to transform Cipriani's for the National Design Awards, hosted by the Cooper-Hewitt, we not only had to find a way to fill the same large physical space again, we needed to do it in a way that made the most of this nonprofit's budget so that the look evoked admiration for its style, not glitz, and ingenuity over ostentation. The monetary limitations were further put to the test by the schedule for the evening, which called for a cocktail party for five hundred, followed by a seated dinner and then an awards show and entertainment. That didn't mean we had to skip on the wow factor, however. Indeed, a tight budget is sometimes the best motivator for making the most of a design challenge.

An incredibly simple decorative device that nonetheless offers limitless possibilities came to the rescue—ribbon. It may be humble, but with the right touch it can transform a room. If you don't have a lot of money, it's important that you don't scatter your resources trying to buy a lot of something cheap. Instead, concentrate your funds on a few fabulous design devices that provide plenty of return for dollars spent. Never water down a design. Instead, take a little and do a lot.

The inspiration for the ribbon look came from the event's invitation, which featured a very linear abstract pattern. That two-dimensional representation became our three-dimensional interpretation. The ribbon theme began right at the venue's entry, which featured an enormous, see-through partition that suspended the sponsor's name upon a web of grosgrain. Through it, guests could spy a forest of ribbons visually slicing the room into thin vertical slats of space.

Party décor is not about filling up the center of tables, or the walls, or the stage, or any part of the space with something simply for the sake of filling it. Construct a conceptual idea in your head and then execute it with all the excellence you can muster. A party's design should be an experience—an experience you not only see, but feel to your core.

NATIONAL DESIGN AWARDS

A large screen serving as the stage backdrop reinforced the crisscross motif—another two-dimensional echo against the three-dimensional décor, that underscores the abstract power of the design.

The ribbon created a modern, sleek interpretation of the classic party streamer; its silken finish and thin elegance provided a stunning presence that easily held its own in a cavernous, powerful party space.

WE turned Cipriani's sky-high ceiling into a décor asset when we created a party for New Yorkers for Children, an organization that assists the education goals of youth placed in foster care. By integrating the night's "Launch a Star" theme, we matched a potent metaphor with the drama of the space.

We began by bathing the ceiling in dark-blue lights that saturated the overhead area to create the sensation of a night sky. Theatrical gobos—bright spotlights covered with templates that project any desired design in the color of your choice—sprinkled the ceiling with a shimmering galaxy of stars. To accentuate the upward message, a ladder cut at an extreme angle suggested the notion that those stars could well be within reach for the children the charity was helping.

While "Starry Night" is a common party theme, we made it fresh. Stars themselves are beauteous, perennial design linchpins. To escape being cliché, we focused on something far more grand than party design—a theme that allowed us to revel in the sheer beauty of stars twinkling high and happily above the guests, each shining dot representing an individual child's promise.

THE SOUL OF THE PARTY

A party is about joy and celebration and bringing people together to share in them. Hosts that embrace that edict from a party's inception through its planning and installation, from the arrival of the first guest until the last straggler goes home, and dedicate themselves to enjoying themselves stack the odds of a successful event in their favor. If a party causes you to worry or panic, you're missing the point!

It's not good when you forget the mini beef Wellington hors d'oeuvres in the oven, but your guests will only give a fig if you do. Channel that nervous energy into making the best of every situation. Energy is what guests remember.

We once discovered—at the reception hall—that a wedding cake had suffered a rather substantial dent in transit. One response would have been to snap at the staff and wring our hands, all the while stinking up the joint with one terribly toxic vibe. The better solution is to get a grip and realize that if the worst thing that happens in your married life is a dented wedding cake, then you're going to have a pretty good marriage. And that's exactly what we told the bride and groom as we discreetly moved the cake next to a wall and rotated the dent to the back—Hey, everybody's got a good side! Dents happen. Deal and move on. Remember that guests follow your cue—relax and your guests will relax.

Parties invite stress because they're live theater—no retakes, no editing, no stunt doubles. As every actor from the community playhouse to the Globe knows full well, the show must go on! Gloss smoothly over a flub and your audience will be none the wiser.

A destination wedding we planned for a couple who shared a passionate love for Istanbul revealed the very essence of what we think it means to discover the soul of a party. Though neither bride nor groom is of Turkish descent, the magic and mystery of that ancient city held such an allure for them that they wanted to share it with friends and family on their momentous occasion, so it was off to that seductive metropolis for a fantasy. The event was a success because, from beginning to end, the hosts put all their energies into to delivering an unforgettably pleasurable evening for their closest and dearest.

When you already have a spectacular or exotic location, look to the excitement that's right at your fingertips first, then lasso it to suit your needs and desires. The embrace of Istanbul's incredible landscape illustrates one of the most important party rules: don't disguise your space, relate to it. If your party's in Grandma's barn in Ohio, work with it! Think hootenanny, or Sadie Hawkins, or any other fun theme that fits. Every element of this celebration—the décor, the music, the food—related to its surroundings and helped cement the night as a memory that would last a lifetime, not just for the newlyweds but for every guest.

Prior to the dinner, there was a sunset yacht cruise on the Bosporus, taking in such sights as the magnificent Blue Mosque. With that tour still fresh in their minds and with that stunning landscape as the backdrop, arriving dinner guests were escorted by a ceremonial drum corps dressed in native garb of fiery-red robes and tall, stiff caps along a waterfront edged with an eclectic string of lanterns and fire pots atop slender metal poles. Spontaneously, sparked by the entrancing mood, some guests rattled tambourines and clicked castanets, adding their own personal touch to the alluring sounds.

As dark crept in, with the architectural icons of Istanbul glowing in the distance, guests stepped into an enormous tent that replicated the interior of a genie's bottle as exotic as any Aladdin ever saw. A ceiling festooned with dozens of different lanterns, each more beautiful than the one before, created a gentle firmament over dinner festivities. A gentle, cheery light suffused the room and played softly off tables covered in vivid red tablecloths and small treasures from the Grand Bazaar.

In the evening's embrace, reeling to the rhythms of arabesque, the brilliantly attired guests melded into the festivities with the giddy entrancement of a whirling dervish, the verve and splash of their every sway and swirl personifying the very definition of party as experience.

Surrounded by the very real elixir of Istanbul's smells, sights, and sounds, the party welcomed two hundred guests with an immersion into sensual delight.

Guests arrived at the sunset rehearsal dinner on the banks of the Bosporus via a grand yacht that oozed local color—literally—with the repeating image of a carnation, a Turkish symbol of hospitality and welcome, splashed across a painted dance floor edged by tightly woven Turkish carpets.

A nearby restaurant's star chef catered the feast, with cuisine rooted in centuries of cooking traditions drawn from the many cultures that have come together in this flamboyant city, such as quince dusted in cinnamon and ice cream sweetened with rose water. Mid-dinner a troupe of belly dancers came undulating onto center stage, entertainment as delectable as the kabobs spiced with preserved lemons. This served as a moment to get dinner guests on their feet—to applaud the meal and encourage them to surrender themselves to the music and the energy.

Delights straight from *1001 Arabian Nights* permeated the entire affair. All the decorative elements for the party itself were inspired and sourced in the famed Egyptian Spice Market and Grand Bazaar. In the midst of cocktail hour, local musicians and a troupe of Turkish folk dancers took to the floor to bewitch the guests with the signature side-by-side moves of centuries-old dances.

Encouraged by the professional performers, guests soon joined in the fun, steadily assembling outside under the starry firmament on the dance floor that had previously served as the cocktail lounge.

WHEN THE PARTY LASTS ALL SEASON LONG

AMERICA's best-kept party secret, like many of the nation's best-kept secrets, can be found at the U.S. Department of State in Washington. Every year during the winter holiday season, a series of reception halls at the department's Foggy Bottom headquarters transform into party spaces that entertain thousands of guests in a steady progression of celebratory lunches, evening soirées, and glittering revelry befitting our diplomatic corps.

When the State Department partnered with Time, Inc. and *InStyle* and its editor Ariel Foxman to create the holiday décor for these rooms, they brought me in to design one look that would be relevant for many types of events.

These spaces are the only parts of the State Department building open to the public—and only during the holidays. We were amazed at how many events the department hosts between the last weeks of November and first weeks of January, and the enormous amount of foot traffic the parties bring. Those weeks offer a veritable cornucopia of festivities as everyone from the Secretary of State to diplomats to agency heads to families of armed forces personnel stationed overseas share in the joy of the season with guests from around the world.

Time, Inc., and *InStyle* provided the resources to turn these stately halls into holiday fantasies of holiday joy—no taxpayer dollars needed. Our participation called for us to create and install décor in six of the department's reception rooms that would have universal appeal, be appropriate to each room, and be able to withstand the rigors of many parties over many weeks. This offered us a chance to tap into *InStyle*'s glam aesthetic and its reputation as a chic, international arbiter of taste and couple them with our style.

We also wanted to honor the these historic rooms—some of the finest museum spaces in America—and this department—the nation's oldest federal agency—but with modernity and innovation. Since we were dealing with the government, every design decision had to pass many layers of approval. And those were only the start of our logistical design parameters. Our décor needed to be mobile, so that any bit of installation could be quickly dismantled and then restaged, depending on the demands of an evening or event.

In one room, for example, we packed a long center table with a lavish bounty of holiday memorabilia to create a visual treasure trove in browns and whites. This was a favorite room for Secretary of State Hillary Clinton's luncheons, however, meaning the room had to easily make way for makeovers, so we placed the items on trays for quick removal and reinstallation. Every decorative element had to be free-standing or supported by its own armature that leaned, rested, or was suspended within the room—no nails allowed! In one case, an archway of shiny gifts that adorned an entry appeared to be built directly into the wall but was, instead, a trellis packed tight with wrapped boxes.

The longevity of the holiday season also meant creating durable décor. We typically create props to last for a six-hour stint and don't relax until an event's last guest has left. Rethinking and reimagining the notion of an 'event' in weeks, not hours, was a challenge all by itself. Fact is, six weeks is a long time to hold your breath.

The rooms' historical import pushed us to strike a balance between a modern take on a party and immense solemnity. Our elements, such as a tree crafted from mirrors that reflected the room's surroundings, sought to respect the classical proportions and styles of the rooms while offering a fresh interpretation on holiday decorations.

The State Department's long history means its storage vault holds
thousands of antiques; having
the opportunity to prowl those
archives to select many of the
items used in the installations
was as close as I've ever come to
feeling like a kid in a candy shop.

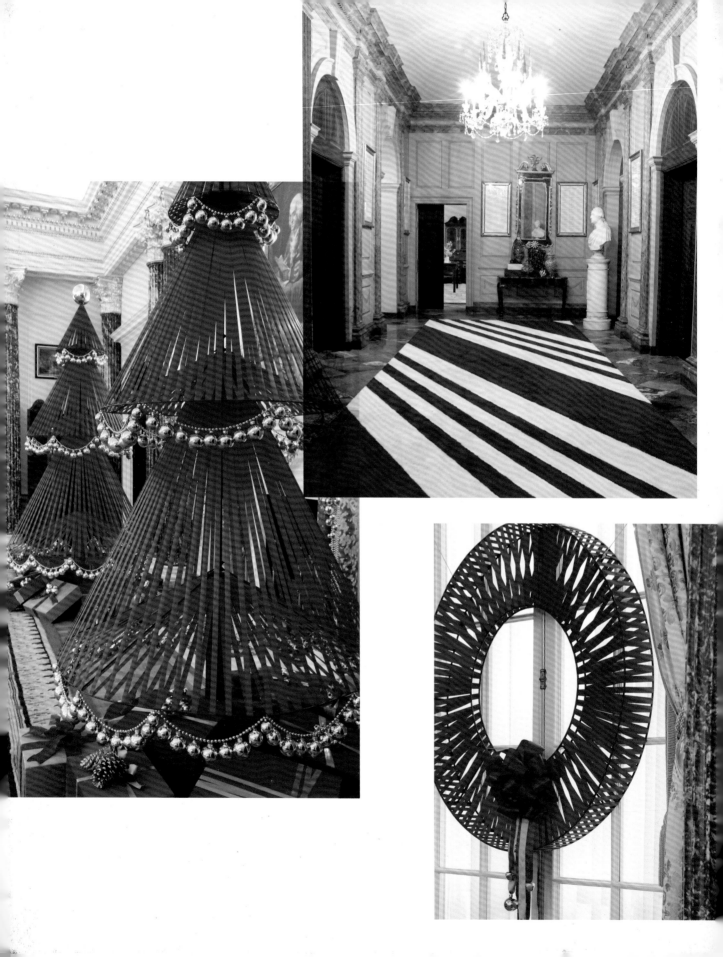

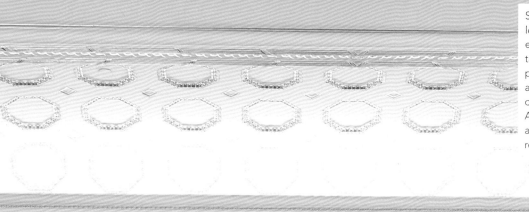

Several of our designs used long lengths of simple ribbon to spin enormous ribbon wreaths and tall holiday trees. By twisting and pulling a single length of ribbon around a prefabricated armature, our designs evoked traditional Americana design, and were achievable for an incredibly reasonable budget.

GOOD BYE

Acknowledgments

Putting together a book is not unlike creating an event: it's all about teamwork. In that spirit, I offer to the entire team—past and present—at David Stark Design and Production my heartfelt thanks, deepest respect, and abiding appreciation for your devotion, passion, energy, and commitment to pushing the boundaries to ever-new and fantastic horizons. This book is a testament to your genius. I dedicate it to you.

Countless hours—sometimes decades!—of teamwork have brought us to a proud moment, evidenced in this volume created with the invaluable contributions of my colleagues Dani Calkins, Christopher Clark, and Susie Montagna.

I am especially proud to call so many of my professional collaborators friends, starting with my agent Carla Mayer Glasser, who brought us together with Stacee Lawrence and her team at the Monacelli Press, including Elizabeth White and Heather Kirkpatrick.

Thanks also to John Morse, the book's writer, Karen Hsu of the design firm Omnivore, and photographers Susie Montagna, Gustavo Campos, Aaron Delesie, Rick Collins, Arnold Brower, Daria Bishop, Brian Dorsey, Heidi Ehalt, KT Merry, Andre Maier, Joe Kohen, John Parra, Rebecca Weiss and Billy Farrell. Thank you fellow artists.

I am grateful to our clients—corporate, nonprofit, and private—who allow me to channel their essence through events that constantly take me on new journeys. I don't decorate. I design. And it is their inspiration that allows me to design who and what they are through my head, heart, and hands.

As a service company, we work with many professionals, including countless lighting designers, tenting companies, caterers, fabricators, musicians, and engineers that provide a net beneath the high-wire acts portrayed in this book. Thank you all.

We are particularly honored to count the wonderful folks at *Martha Stewart Weddings* as colleagues. We cherish our collaborations with them, some of which can be seen on pages 8–23 and 72–85. We also thank our friends at Paul Wilmot Communications who work so hard to get our work out into the world, including Jessica Ritt, Becky Levin, Lauran Claps, Paul Wilmot, Hampton Carney, and Kate Doerge.

Thank you to my parents for the ceaseless support that has allowed me to become the artist I am.

Finally, a special thank you to Migguel Anggelo, whose support, love, and creativity are food for the soul. Thank you for the banquet.